Hegel and the State

Translated by Mark A. Cohen

Eric Weil

*Hegel and the State*

❧ ❧ ❧ ❧ ❧ ❧

The Johns Hopkins University Press

*Baltimore and London*

Originally published as *Hegel et l'Etat: Cinq conférences suivies de "Marx et la philosophie du droit"* by Librairie Philosophique J. Vrin, 1950. © Vrin 1985

English translation © 1998 The Johns Hopkins University Press
All rights reserved. Published 1998
Printed in the United States of America on acid-free paper

9  8  7  6  5  4  3  2  1

The Johns Hopkins University Press
2715 North Charles Street
Baltimore, Maryland 21218–4363
The Johns Hopkins Press Ltd., London
www.press.jhu.edu

Library of Congress Cataloging-in-Publication Data will be found at the end of this book.
A catalog record for this book is available from the British Library.

ISBN 0-8018-5865-8

# Contents

# Preface

This book is entitled *Hegel and the State*. But the title does not give an entirely accurate idea of its scope. In fact, it proposes a critique of the orthodox critique, which has depicted Hegel as an apologist for the Prussian State and a prophet of what is often called statism. Is this critique valid? If the State forms the centerpiece of his political theory, should we automatically deem a philosopher unworthy of our interest? And even if we assume that such a critical attitude is correct, should it apply to Hegel?

Given my topic, then, readers who are looking for a comprehensive analysis of Hegel's philosophy of the State in these pages will be disappointed. For such an undertaking to be successful it would have to start with Hegel's ontology—his *onto-logic,* the indispensable basis for understanding all the elements of his system—whereas the goals of this work rule out any discussion and interpretation of his politics (in the Aristotelian sense) relying on notions immanent to the Hegelian system itself. Nevertheless, readers will come across occasional allusions to it in what follows, and as a result I hope they will acknowledge that a genuine attempt has been made to respect the unity of Hegel's thought.

I have also forgone any attempt to provide a critical survey of current Hegelian scholarship. There are a few references to contemporary works on Hegel in the footnotes, but they are not intended to refute or emend their arguments in any detail—such details are not my concern here. Scholars well versed in Hegel's system will not have any trouble finding points with which to agree or disagree in what follows because, unless I am very much mistaken, they will quickly realize that I have not really challenged the reigning orthodoxy except in deciding which texts of the Hegelian corpus are reliable. I have used only those that were written in the period following the defeat of Napoleon, so there are no references here to Hegel's early writings or, with a few exceptions, to the *Phenomenology of Spirit.* My work has been concentrated mainly on the *Philosophy of Right* and to a lesser degree on the *Encyclopedia of the Philosophical Sciences.* Those texts not written directly by Hegel himself—most importantly, the *Additions* to the *Philosophy of Right,* which the editors of the *Collected Works* adapted from their teacher's lectures, the *Lectures on the Philosophy of History,* and the *Lectures on the History of Philosophy*—have only been used for the purpose of furnishing illustrations or formulations of ideas that can be found in the main texts, and even then only when these subsidiary sources seemed reliably authentic.[1] It is thus obvious that any discussion of the development of Hegel's thought is out of the question. This theme has already been taken up by Th. L. Haering and, before him and in a superior treatment, by F. Rosenzweig in a work that is notable for the perspicuity it displays in its treatment of individual problems but in my opinion is mistaken in its overall conception of the issue.[2]

1. Of course, I do not wish to claim that the texts taken from Hegel's various lectures are utterly worthless for the interpretation of his thought. But too often they have served as the basic material of interpretation, and their formulations of important ideas, which lose in precision as they gain in forcefulness, have therefore done more harm than good. The only authoritative text should be the one that the author has published in its final form after lengthy reflection and the painstaking process of composition, procedures that are not available to even the most accomplished orator speaking extemporaneously (as was Hegel's practice). Wherever the "Lectures" seem to contradict the published books and writings we must follow the latter, and wherever they agree the former will not teach us anything new (except where they offer applications of the system to heretofore unexamined domains). It is more legitimate and less complicated to restrict ourselves solely to those texts published by Hegel himself.

2. Th. L. Haering, *Hegel, sein Wollen und sein Werk,* 2 vols. (Leipzig and Berlin, 1929–38); Fr. Rosenzweig, *Hegel und der Staat,* 2 vols. (Munich and Berlin, 1920). It would be impossible to list all the interpretations that have been made of Hegel's political philosophy. Few authors who deal with either modern history, the theory of the State, or nineteenth-century political movements have not devoted at least

I have also thought it worthwhile to add a brief appendix, "Marx and the Philosophy of Right."

❋  ❋  ❋

In an age that prefers passion to thinking—for reasons Hegel so accurately pointed out—it is certainly permissible to add a short postscript concerning the goals of the present work. I am well aware that Hegel can manage very well without defenders: if Hegel's theory is correct, reality itself will ensure that its validity is confirmed. I know that seeking to make the theory more accessible would be equally pointless; one does not rewrite scientific books for popular consumption.[3] No one doubts the signal value of providing a detailed and continuous commentary in order to facilitate the task of reading (which it is not possible to do here), but that does not entail translating the text into "clearer" and more concise language. On the contrary, a philosophical work susceptible of being translated in this way would not merit the attempt. In a philosophical text each individual sentence is as important for understanding the whole as each individual formula in a mathematical treatise—which we would not dream of transcribing into "plain" English or cutting down by half so as not to overburden the reader. A work such as this can have no other aim than to stimulate interest in the text as it stands and to remove any hindrances to its comprehension that have accumulated over time.

----

some space to it. References to the most important works before 1920 are given by Rosenzweig. More recent bibliographies can be found in Henri Niel, *De la médiation dans la philosophie de Hegel* (Paris, 1945); and Jean Hyppolite, *Génèse et structure de la Phénoménologie de l'Esprit de Hegel* (Paris, 1947). For English-language bibliographies see G. H. Sabine, *A History of Political Theory* (London, 1948); and W. M. McGovern's more complete *From Luther to Hitler* (Boston, 1941). In France the debate appears to have progressed very little beyond E. Vermeil's summation and criticism of the opposing theses of Andler and Basch in "La Pensée politique de Hegel," in *Études sur Hegel* (Paris, 1931), 165–234.

3. [I have retained the French word *science* here and throughout where *philosophical* would be more immediately appropriate. Both the French word *science* and the German *Wissenschaft* can be used for the whole area of human knowledge rather than simply the natural sciences as *science* by itself tends to do in English. TRANS.]

I am fully conscious that my endeavor will arouse universal indignation, that is, if it causes any reaction at all. The reasons for this judgment will vary considerably. There will be those who say that the interpretation (or counterinterpretation) I propose serves to justify a dictatorship of the Left, or the Right, or liberalism, moralism, indifferentism, dogmatism, and so on. Whatever their differences, they will all agree on one thing: that the book should be condemned. I do not plead innocent to the charges—even though I feel that I have every right to do so—because I know that my chance of being acquitted is rather slim. The only right I do claim (and for safety's sake I shall avail myself of it immediately) is to stress that I am presenting a *scientific* thesis about a *scientific* book, that what I say (and what I claim Hegel has said) is either true or false, and that I cannot stop to consider the advisability or consequences of my conclusions. Science, in whatever form it takes, does not tell us to do one thing or another. This is especially true of philosophy, which should not be included among the sciences only because it is science to a greater degree than any of the others, science in the purest sense. Indeed it is philosophy that imbues any interest attaching to a particular science with its essentially *scientific* character (although we experience the interest in ignorance of the fact). Science says that "*if* you want this, you have to do that or accept this"; or "*if* you adopt such a position, it will require of you response $x$ in the face of difficulty $y$." It does not tell you what you should do and is even sufficiently liberal to accept a course of action that might lead to its own destruction. In this instance, though persons of science might then voice their opposition to it, since they have chosen to live their lives by science's values, they will stress that their reaction merely represents their own unscientific opinion. For its part, science serves everyone equally but refuses its services when someone wants it to function exclusively for their own ends.

When I choose to discuss the State *in itself*, or History *in itself*, or Society *in itself*, this will only anger those who fabricate "systems" (whose abiding characteristic is their incoherence). Yet to do so is perhaps the most truly political task of all. It may well be that reason cannot accomplish anything without passion. But it will always be worthwhile, not to say indispensable, since we excuse ourselves from doing it so easily, to ask how passion and reason are related, a dilemma that falls squarely within reason's jurisdiction.

It is certainly possible that Hegel was wrong. It is just as likely— and I think this is probably closer to the truth—that his basic thesis cannot be refuted, though it remains vulnerable to obsolescence; that is, it could be preserved in its essential lineaments while demanding expansion and development in certain areas. After all, over the course of one hundred and thirty years of turbulent historical events and changes we have been confronted with problems that no one could have predicted in Hegel's day, at least not in detail. Whatever the case, my intention here is not to take a position on a specific issue but to discuss the rational foundations for taking a position, for any taking of a position that is conscious, responsible, and coherent—in short, truly political.

E. W.

Hegel and the State

## Chapter One

# The Historical Context of Hegel's Political Philosophy

Despite the large number of excellent books on Hegel that have appeared over the course of the last thirty years in Germany as well as France, Hegel is the least familiar of all the major philosophers, or rather, the most misunderstood. This has not prevented a definitive image of him from becoming firmly entrenched in the popular imagination. All great thinkers tend to leave a similarly stereotypical portrait of themselves behind. Their historical importance resides precisely in the fact that the image of them we have retained functions more as a simplified ideal than as a rational concept. Just as Plato is known as the inventor of the Ideas and of Platonic love, Aristotle as the father of formal logic and biology, Descartes as the champion of clarity, and Kant as the strictest of moralists, Hegel is known as the philosopher for whom the State is everything, the individual nothing, and morality a lower form of the life of the spirit—nothing more or less than the great apologist of the Prussian State.

It is of course common knowledge that Hegel dealt with many other philosophical problems, that he was what is often termed a panlogicist, that he produced what has been declared a completely unintelligible, "romantic," and—still more reprehensible—unscientific philosophy of nature, that he gave lectures on the philosophy of religion, aesthetics, and history. It is equally well known that his works have often been immensely influential, whether directly or in the way they shaped the thought of writers who were developing their own philosophies in opposition to the conclusions reached by Hegel (thereby adhering almost unconsciously to his basic formulation of the problems treated). It would not be wrong to say that even though they were trying to refute his ideas, these adversaries were still using Hegelian categories to do so. But these are nothing more than faded memories gleaned from the history of philosophy. The hard currency now circulating among the reading public (which ultimately means the public pure and simple) has been stamped with the face of the true Prussian, the reactionary, the implacable foe of the "liberals," the personification of all that was most reprehensible and detestable in the eyes of the many groups making up the "Left" in the nineteenth century. It would be the height of folly to challenge such an image.

Still, there can be no question that an attempt to do so could easily be justified by a simple examination of the evidence. For instance, the first thing Hegel did on turning away from his youthful absorption in theological questions and becoming interested in political issues was to become one of Prussia's harshest critics.[1] It is therefore legiti-

---

1. It is not Hegel but Fichte who at a certain point in his career merits the title "philosopher of the Prussian State," if by that one means a police State, run by governmental decree and governed by a centralized and absolute authority. Hegel consistently voiced his utter contempt for the State's attempt to regulate everything down to the most insignificant details of everyday existence starting with his first published work, *Differenz des Fichte'schen und Schelling'schen Systems* (1801), ed. G. Lasson (Leipzig, 1928), 64 ff. and 67n, and continuing all the way to the *Philosophie des Rechts* (1821), ed. G. Lasson, 2d ed. (Leipzig, 1921), xiv ff. The text of the *Constitution* proves that Hegel's resistance to Frederician and post-Frederician autocracy was a matter of philosophical as well as emotional conviction (*Die Verfassung Deutschlands* [The German constitution], in *Schriften zur Politik und Rechtsphilosophie,* ed. G. Lasson, 2d ed. [Leipzig, 1923]):

There is an infinite difference between a State authority *[Staatsgewalt]* that is so constituted that everything on which it can rely is found in itself and that, conversely and precisely because of this, can rely on nothing else and [a State authority] that in addition to what it has at its own disposal can also rely on the free adhesion, the pride *[Selbstgefühl]*, and the activity of the people itself, on an all powerful and invincible spirit that this hierarchy drove out and that survives only where the supreme authority leaves the greatest possible amount of freedom to the citizens' own initiative *[Besorgung]*. It will only become clear in the future how in a modern State where

mate to argue that the Prussia he was attacking at this time had not yet become the one he would later hold up as exemplary[2] and that it is his *first* and earlier image of Prussia that fits our customary notions of what that State was like. In support of this assumption we can add that historical Prussia, the Prussia of Frederick William IV, of the Williams, the Prussia that formed the heart of the Third Reich, apparently felt no debt of gratitude to its "philosopher." On the contrary, immediately after his death the royal government did all it could to root out his influence by summoning the aged Schelling to Berlin and denying Hegelians professorships. It is remarkable that with the July Revolution of 1830 Hegel's political philosophy started to have an enormous influence in every corner of the globe—everywhere, that is, except Prussia. We can deduce from this that in reality the Prussian State did not recognize itself in the image that Hegel supposedly painted of it, either because his portrayal was inaccurate or because he had captured its features only too well.[3]

----

everything is regulated from the top down, where nothing that possesses a universal aspect is left to the administration and execution of those elements of the people whose concerns are involved—this is the form the French Republic took—[how in such a State] a desiccated and tedious [literally, "made of leather"] life without spirit will result if this pedantic tone of government persists. But what sort of life and desiccation prevails in another State, governed in the same manner—in Prussia—will strike anyone who enters the first village he finds or sees its complete lack of scientific and artistic genius or does not gauge its strength according to the ephemeral energy with which an isolated genius was able to galvanize it for a short time. (31)

This article was never completed, but there is general agreement that it was written sometime between 1798 and 1802.

2. See the texts cited below.

3. He captured it only too well for the liking of a romantic such as Frederick William, who was a great admirer of the theories of C. L. von Haller (see below) and was not amused when someone insisted that post-Napoleonic Prussia was a constitutional State, at least in theory. On the other hand, the *Philosophy of Right* could just as easily be construed as "inaccurate" because Hegel imputes to Prussia a number of features and institutions that for him are essential but never existed there or, if they did, existed only in those territories restored to it in 1815. Since I am not writing a history, three examples of the difference between his description and the reality will suffice:

First, the entire structure of the Hegelian State is based on and centered around a

All of this contradicts the widespread tradition that holds Hegel to be the philosopher of the Restoration. But merely pointing it out will certainly not be enough to render the image to which I have just referred obsolete, although I should state from the outset that I think this image is totally inaccurate. Even if the above objections are substantially correct, even if Hegel's admiration for Prussia could not possibly have been a matter of emotional and unthinking reflex given the disapproval he displayed for it from the outset of his career, and even if the hostility of the Prussian State toward him demonstrates that his admiration could not have been unconditional, a number of remarks of at least equal weight point in the opposite direction: he described the Prussian State as the perfect form of the State; he pro-

---

parliament (the estates = *Stände,* in the same sense that the word *estates* had in 1789, although the estates Hegel is referring to were not identical to the latter), but there was no parliament in Prussia, only provincial estates, and what is more, the first meeting of these provincial estates in a Prussian "diet" did not take place until 1847. To do Hegel justice I should note that he displayed a good deal of courage in his lectures, for Frederick William III, having promised in a cabinet order issued on 22 May 1815 that a "representative body of the people" would be created, took it amiss when he was reminded of his promise. On 21 March 1818 his response to those Rhenish provincial and communal authorities who had dared to call for a constitution was as follows: "Neither the edict of 22 May 1815 nor article 13 of the act of Confederation specifies the time when the constitution by estates must be introduced. The time for making changes to the constitution of the State cannot be chosen without careful consideration. Whoever reminds the sovereign of promises he made entirely of his own free will and by his own decision is impiously and criminally displaying doubt in the character of the promise of the prince and usurps the judgment of the latter regarding the proper time for the introduction of this constitution."

Second, open parliamentary debates were not permitted in the provinces that had retained estates. But according to Hegel, such open debate was vital for the public supervision of the government and for the formation of public opinion.

Third, the jury was an institution that had never existed in the Prussia of the ancien régime, but according to Hegel, nothing else could satisfy the self-consciousness of the citizen, who demands to be judged by his peers and not by a corporation foreign to him.

Moreover, readers of the *Philosophy of Right* do not need to delve into scholarly works specializing in the matter to ascertain to what extent historical Prussia corresponded to what Hegel called a modern State in 1815–20; they can simply read the chapter devoted to Prussia in Charles Seignobos's *Histoire politique de l'Europe contemporaine, évolution des partis et des formes politiques, 1814–1896* (Paris, 1897).

claimed that the Germano-Christian spirit was the dominant force in modern history; and he criticized English plans for parliamentary reform in 1830, contrasting them with the political conditions that had been established by the government in Berlin.[4] This is strong evidence, all the more convincing because it comes from Hegel's own lips. There can be no doubt that Hegel can at least be described as an admirer of the *principle* of the Prussian State. How we are to interpret this admiration remains an open question.

❋ ❋ ❋

In my survey of the literature devoted to Hegel in the second half of the nineteenth century I found only a single text—barely even a text, really, nothing more than a few passages scattered over various letters—that undertakes to defend him against the traditional charge that he was a reactionary philosopher.[5] With this sole exception, all sides are in complete agreement. Take the old liberal Haym,[6] not

4. See below for further references.

5. In the interests of accuracy, some other apologies for Hegel should be included, such as that of Rosenkranz, *Apologie Hegels gegen R. Haym* (Berlin, 1858). Apart from the fact that this piece is rather weak, despite a good number of discerning and pertinent observations, its author (like E. Gans) belonged to the Hegelian school, which soon found itself forced onto the defensive and by the middle of the nineteenth century had lost whatever influence it once enjoyed. The history of the Hegelian movement still remains to be written, the best summary available being that of Johann Eduard Erdmann, *Grundriss der Geschichte der Philosophie*, 3d ed. (Berlin, 1878), §§ 331 ff. (the fourth edition, written by *Benno* Erdmann, is unusable). The manner in which the Greater German tradition of our century judges Hegel can be clearly gauged in Friedrich Meinecke's (Rosenzweig's teacher) vindication of Hegel's philosophy: "Conservative, liberal, and radical thinkers, historicists and doctrinaires, nationalist and cosmopolitans should all be instructed in this system . . . He [Hegel] is among the first rank of the great nineteenth-century thinkers who have elucidated the signification of the State [*Staatsgesinnung*] for the general public, that is, the conviction of the greatness and the moral dignity of the State" (*Weltbürgertum und Nationalstaat*, 2d ed. [Munich and Berlin, 1911], 272). In other words, Hegel is not as anti-Prussian as is commonly believed, although that does not make him any less of a universalist (Meinecke says this on 278). The nationalist Meinecke ends up concurring with the liberal Haym.

6. Of all Hegel's opponents, Rudolph Haym is by far the most important, as much

to mention thinkers of lesser stature, if not less influential, such as Welcker and Rotteck, who were leading figures of the constitutional party of Greater Germany. Or on the extreme Left, the Bauers and their followers. Their verdict is unanimous.[7] When we look at the Right—which is always made up of people who feel that they have finally understood the eternal truth—that is, to Schelling, the heirs of Romanticism, or the Historical School, led by Savigny, we find that they did not consider Hegel a kindred spirit because they felt that he had not kept up with the times and had failed to grasp the aspirations of a reinvigorated epoch that had purged itself of the disorders that had plagued the eighteenth century.[8] As a result, in their opinion too Hegel was a man of the past.

One exception to these negative views is an article on Hegel that appeared in a periodical. Since the date was 1870 and Hegel had been forgotten in Germany, the editor thought it necessary to add a note to the effect that Hegel was famous as the man who had discovered and glorified the "royal-Prussian" idea. On reading this the author of the article flew into a rage and wrote to a common friend: "That dumb brute took the liberty of adding footnotes to my article without any indication that they were not mine, and what they say is utterly idiotic. I had already made my objections known some time ago, but nowadays stupidity flows so thick that things can't possibly go on like this much longer . . . That dumb brute who for years has stuck to the ridiculous opposition of law and power and not managed to get beyond it, like a foot soldier who has been put on a wild horse and left

---

for the high quality of his book about Hegel as for its subsequent influence. His *Hegel und seine Zeit* (Hegel and his times) was a product of the reactionary period that followed the defeat of the 1848 Revolution. The appendixes of a second edition (Leipzig, 1927), prepared by H. Rosenberg, provide useful pointers for assessing both Haym's own development and the history of Hegelianism.

7. But see above, n. 5. For the young Marx's critique see the appendix at the end of this book.

8. A great deal of information (without any comprehension of the underlying philosophical issues) can be found in M. Lenz's three-part *Geschichte der Universität Berlin,* 4 vols. (Halle, 1910–18). This work provides a convenient guide to the development of governmental policy and university opinion in the nineteenth century.

in the coral, this ignoramus has the nerve to try and dismiss a man like Hegel with the word 'Prussian' . . . I've had enough . . . It's better not to be published than to look like an ass." To which his correspondent replied by return of post: "I have written to him that it would be better to shut up than to repeat Rotteck and Welckers' old nonsense . . . this fellow really is too stupid." The poor editor is Wilhelm Liebknecht, one of the leading figures of German social democracy, the author of the first letter is Engels, and the response comes from Marx.[9]

9. Friedrich Engels to Karl Marx, 8 May 1870, and Marx to Engels, 10 May 1870, Letters 329 and 331 in *Collected Works* vol. 43, *1868–70* (New York, 1988), 508–9, 511 [the English translations of the German given below are from this text. TRANS.].The original from which my somewhat toned down translation is taken reads:

Mit Monsieur Wilhelm ist es nicht zum Aushalten. Du wirst gesehen haben wie "durch Abwesenheit des Setzers" (der also der eigentliche Redakteur ist) der Bauernkrieg in einem Durcheinander gedruckt wird, das Grandperret nicht besser machen könnte, [Monsieur Wilhelm is no longer to be borne. You will have seen that "owing to the absence of the printer" (who is, thus, the real editor), the *Peasant War* was printed in a mix-up that Grandperret could not have managed better; *Weil begins here.* TRANS.] und dabei untersteht sich das Vieh, mir Randglossen ohne jede Angabe des Verfassers drunter zu setzen, die reiner Blödsinn sind, und die *Jedermann mir zuschreiben muss.* Ich habe es mir schon einmal verbeten und tat es pikiert, jetzt kommt der Blödsinn aber so dick, daß es nicht länger geht. [*Weil leaves the next lines untranslated.* TRANS.] Der Mensch glossiert ad vocem Hegel: dem größern Publikum bekannt als Entdecker (!) und Vererrlicher (!!) der königlich preußischen *Staatsidee* (!!!!). Ich habe ihm hierauf nun gehörig gedient und ihm eine, unter den Umständen möglichst milde Erklärung zum Abdruck zugeschickt. [*Ad vocem* Hegel, the fellow glosses: known to the general public as the discoverer (!) and glorifier (!!) of the royal Prussian *state concept* (!!!!). I have retorted to him suitably, and have sent him, for publication, a declaration as mild as was possible; *Weil picks up the translation here.* TRANS.] Dieses Vieh, das Jahrelang auf dem lächerlichen Gegensatz von Recht und Macht hülflos herumgeritten wie ein Infanterist, den man auf ein kolleriges Pferd gesetzt und in der Reitbahn eingeschloßen hat—dieser Ignorant hat die Unverschämtheit, einen Kerl wie Hegel mit dem Wort: "Preuss" abfertigen zu wollen und dabei dem Publikum weiszumachen, ich hätte das gesagt. Ich bin das Ding jetzt satt. [*Weil omits the next line.* TRANS.] Wenn W. meine Erklärung nicht druckt, so wende ich mich an seine Vorgesetzten, den "Ausschuß", und wenn die auch Manöver machen, so verbiete ich den Weiterdruck. [If Wilhelm doesn't publish my declaration, I shall turn to his superiors, the "Committee," and if they also get up to tricks, I shall prohibit any further publication. *Weil picks up the translation here.* TRANS.] Lieber gar nicht gedruckt, als von Wilh. dadurch zum Esel proklamiert" [letter 329]—"Ich hatte ihm geschrieben, wenn er über Hegel nur den alten Rotteck-Welckerschen

This is all rather surprising. Marx and Engels beg to differ from those who proclaim that Hegel glorified the "royal-Prussian" idea of the State, and they call anyone who places Hegel in the same category as the reactionaries a dumb brute. They have traditionally been considered his most severe critics, and here they are defending his political reputation. How can this be explained?

Obviously, the expression of an opinion in a letter is not the same as a definitive refutation, even when it comes from two people as steeped in Hegelian thought as Marx and Engels. Nonetheless, it only serves to confirm our suspicions. Nothing would be more natural than for these self-styled theorists of revolution to repeat the accusations of Hegel's conformism, Prussianism, and conservatism. If the very men who claimed to have superseded Hegel did not see fit to accuse him of

---

Dreck zu wiederholen wisse, so solle er doch lieber das Maul halten. [*Weil omits the next line.* TRANS.] Das nennt er den Hegel "etwas unzeremoniöser ubers Knie bre-chen etc." und wenn er Eseleien unter Engels Aufsätze schreibt, so "Engels kann ja (!) *Ausführliches* (!!) sagen". [He says that this would be "making rather informally short work, etc." of Hegel, and when he writes stupidities beneath Engels' articles, then "Engels can of course (!) say something *at greater length* (!!)." *Weil picks up the translation here.* TRANS.] Der Mensch ist wirklich zu dumm [letter 331].

This letter is interesting for two reasons. On the one hand, it demonstrates the difference between the founders of Marxism and their successors: Liebknecht even-tually won out over Marx and Engels, and as things now stand the "revolutionaries" are in agreement with the "reactionaries" in seeing Hegel as the apologist of the Prussian State. In the most recent work to come from the Marxist school, *Der junge Hegel—Über die Beziehungen von Dialektik und Ökonomie* (The young Hegel— on the relationship of dialectics and political economy)(Zurich and Vienna, 1948), G. Lukács continues to state that since Hegel was an idealist he was incapable of refusing reconciliation with the wretched reality of his time. We should take into account that Lukács limits himself to the *Phenomenology of Spirit* and does not feel obliged to prove by any actual interpretation of the texts those claims he makes on deductive grounds. On the other hand, this work permits us to grasp the reasons for the curious alliance between German "liberals" and "nationalists": the former are defending society against the State, the latter the State against society, and both are refusing to conceive society as part of the State [*penser la société dans l'Etat*], whereas Marx and Engels—for whom the issue was precisely their unity—recognized the philosophical validity of Hegel's analysis and opposed the attempt to set it aside in favor of a dogmatic position employing politically motivated value judgments. For the difference between Hegel and Marx see the appendix to this volume.

these things, how can we avoid asking whether these labels are really justified? And if there is doubt about the traditional image of Hegel, clearly we will have to do more than simply correct a few errors of detail. We will have to replace it with an entirely different image.

There is only one legitimate way of going about this: we should look at the texts themselves and try to understand what Hegel said, what he meant, and then compare the results of our examination with the traditional critique. If the suspicions I have just referred to are confirmed, this tradition will easily be explained as a simple philosophical accident (if not an accident plain and simple). It can be explained in the first instance by Hegel's being a difficult author. It is not that he lacks precision and clarity but rather that achieving precision and clarity in philosophy has the unfortunate consequence of ruling out elegant style or easy reading. Hegel is clear not *despite* the fact that he demands an intense collaboration from his reader but *because* he does.

There is another factor to be considered. Philosophers—and this is what makes them philosophers and not men of action[10]—prefer not to take a position on current political issues because (and this is only paradoxical at first glance) they are trying to understand politics *in general*. Hegel, like Plato or Aristotle, did not take a position on the issues of the day. Just as orthodox Christians as well as deists and atheists appealed to his *Philosophy of Religion,* people with all sorts of different opinions could attack (and sometimes endorse) his political theory precisely because opinions did not matter to him, only theory and science.

Finally, and I bring this up so I will not have to return to it again since it has no bearing on anything essential, Hegel did not always display more courage than most people of his time or any other time. In certain instances he accepted prevailing conditions without demur (e.g., in the case of entailed property, which he was against in principle

10. [This text was written in France in the late 1940s and typically uses *man* and the masculine form of the pronoun in place of *men and women, humanity,* and *person* throughout. TRANS.]

but which he allowed in practice for reasons of "higher political realities" [*haute politique*]). Likewise, he did not always care to elaborate on
those of his views that might arouse the ire (or worse) of the ministry for religious affairs; he preferred to say what he had to say with a
certain amount of discretion, thereby displaying a great deal of faith
in the ability of his contemporary readers, justifiably as it turned out,
not to connect two passages that he had not placed on the same page,
nor to draw conclusions that all the premises, as well as the necessary
method for drawing conclusions from them, had been provided. We
could censure him for not directly challenging the authorities because
he feared the consequences for a man in his position. Let he who is
without sin cast the first stone. But despite such compromises, it seems
that when it came to presenting the essential core of his theory, Hegel
refused to omit even the smallest item necessary for its elaboration.

★ ★ ★

It will be helpful to recall the decisive events shaping the history of
Prussia at the beginning of the nineteenth century, that is, the period
contemporaneous with Hegel's own lifetime.[11] It was an extraordi-
narily turbulent time. Whereas the Revolution had no immediate
effects in Berlin (although it was by no means the case that the whole
of Prussian society was hostile or indifferent to it), the Napoleonic
Wars were to have greater repercussions there than in any of the
other great capitals. The Prussian State ruled by Frederick II, a monarchy equally absolute and perhaps even more centralized than the
Russian Empire, collapsed at Jena, and collapsed all the more rapidly
as a result of the greater purity attained by its principle [*principe*] of
government. In the space of four years Prussia was transformed: land
became alienable (with the sole exception of entailed land), the peas-
ants were freed, the *corvées* abolished within almost all its domains, the
towns given administrative autonomy, the provincial diets allowed
to meet again and reformed, the greater part of the nobility's special

11. For what follows see Seignobos, *Histoire politique de l'Europe contemporaine.*

privileges abolished, intellectual life [*la science*] freed from the direct supervision of the State, and the professional army transformed into a national one. In other words, virtually all the gains of the Revolution were granted to the Prussian people. But it is crucial to note that these changes occurred not because the people rose up and demanded their rights but because the government clearly recognized that only thoroughgoing reform could provide the means for reinvigorating the State, preparing effectively for the coming war, and inspiring the national renewal without which the struggle to defeat Napoleon would not have had the slightest chance of success.[12]

It was natural that after the Allied victory some of these reforms were, if not abrogated, at least applied at a more cautious pace. By acting more to slow down the enforcement of the new program than to return to the old system the privileged orders of the ancien régime regained a number of their traditional prerogatives and a great deal of their social influence once the pressure of external forces had relaxed and brought the need to maintain internal unity to an end. However, it should be added that if the fear of revolution was still very much in the air (in fact after a brief burst of reactionary feeling following the revolutions in Italy and Spain and the assassinations of the Duc de Berry and Kotzebue,[13] a concerted counterrevolutionary program was not put into effect until after the 1830 revolution), and if a certain "authoritarian" and "legitimist" politics came to predominate for all practical purposes (if not as a governing principle), compared with the France of the Restoration, England before the 1832 Reform Bill,

12. This cannot be stressed enough because it fully explains Hegel's confidence in Prussian officials and their knowledge of governmental affairs and problems. But of course it is also little more than a detail of Hegel's biography that explains but does not justify his position. For an analysis of a case in which "enlightened" government and "backward" diet were opposed to each other see "Verhandlungen in der Versammlung der Landstände des Königreichs Württemberg" (Debates in the Assembly of the Provincial Diet of the Kingdom of Württemberg) (1817), in *Schriften zur Politik und Rechtsphilosophie*, 157–280.

13. About the friction between the University of Berlin and the ministry after the Kotzebue-Sand affair and Hegel's attitude toward it see Lenz, *Geschichte der Universität Berlin*.

or the Austria of Metternich, Prussia was by far the more advanced
State. In France the reforms of 1830 brought to 200,000 the number
of electors for the nation as a whole; in Paris under Charles X there
had been no more than 1850. Prussia was not of course a democratic
state in the modern sense; but with its provincial diets, which were
consultative and elected, it was as much one and in a certain sense
more so than, for example, Great Britain.[14] Regarding the latter, in this
period one cannot speak of its having a parliament that represented
the people in any real sense. Even the notion that it was an elected parliament is false: the abolition of the "rotten boroughs" in 1832 would
raise the proportion of eligible voters to the total population from
only 1 in 32 to 1 in 22. While it is true that in Hegel's time the British
Parliament exercised sovereign power over the nation, the people did
not have the power to decide who would be sitting in it. Moreover,
it is beyond dispute that Prussia had by far the more modern administrative apparatus of the two,[15] since it was only with the reforms
begun in 1832 that Great Britain acquired—and even then only at a
snail's pace—a body of law and a system of local and national administration that was not completely controlled by corporate bodies and
the "great families," whereas in its western territories Prussia had preserved all of the institutions originally set up under the Napoleonic
Empire and it undertook the modernization of its other possessions.

It was in the premier university of this renovated Prussia that Hegel
taught, beginning in 1818. He assumed his position with an inaugu-
ral speech in which he paid homage to the State that had appointed

14. It is not without interest to recall that it was only two years after the *Philosophy of Right* was published that Frederick William III instituted the provincial diets
as the sole representatives of the people. In 1821 the Hardenberg Plan called for a
national parliament, and it is quite possible that Hegel meant for his publication to
support this form of representation.

15. [The French term *administration* and its adjectival form refer to the unelected
apparatus of government and combine the functions of *government* and *bureaucracy;*
that is, they are not be confused with the American term since they denote a wider
array of political functions than the executive branch and its appointees. TRANS.]

him.[16] As he saw things, it was a propitious moment for philosophy. Spirit, which had been preoccupied with external matters during the previous period, could now return to its proper domain. Freedom had been preserved, and in this struggle Spirit had risen above particular opinions and interests to attain a profundity that would permit philosophy to live and progress while at the same time protecting it from agnosticism, whether in the form of historicism, sentimentalism, or the critical reflection so beloved of the Kantians. And if the moment was propitious, so was the place. Hegel was speaking in the capital of Prussia, a State that now ranked among the richest and greatest in Europe. Whatever importance it currently possessed in the world and in politics had been achieved with the aid of Spirit. It was in Prussia that the advance of human knowledge had come to constitute one of the essential moments in the life of the State. Prussia was the State of Spirit.[17]

This is not the only place where Hegel makes an explicit reference to Prussia. But there are far fewer occurrences of this sort than one would expect after reading the traditional accounts. In addition to the young Hegel's critique of the Prussian State, mentioned above, other texts also make explicit mention of Prussia, but dating from the Berlin period. In the *Lectures on the Philosophy of History*—one of the compilations we owe to the devotion of Hegel's disciples, hence lacking the authority of the works he published himself—Prussia appears as the representative of the new Church, the Lutheran Church, whose essential character is that it has finally annulled the division between the sacred and the profane. According to Hegel, it was toward this Prussia that the gaze of freedom had turned in the past and would surely turn again.[18]

16. The text precedes the main text in the Lasson edition of Hegel's *Encyclopedia*, 2d ed. (Leipzig, 1920), lxxii ff.

17. [Weil mostly leaves *esprit* (spirit) uncapitalized, but occasionally he capitalizes it for emphasis, as in this paragraph.]

18. In *Vorlesungen über die Philosophie der Weltgeschichte*, ed. G. Lasson, 2d ed., 5 vols.

Finally, there is an implicit reference to Prussia in the famous article "The English Reform Bill,"[19] although it is no more than that since Prussia itself is not actually named. Hegel's intentions in writing this article are debatable: Did he want to warn the English of the risks they were running by undertaking reforms? This is unlikely because the semifeudal character of pre-Reform England was never to Hegel's liking. Did he intend to say that makeshift remedies were inadequate given the seriousness of the present situation? Perhaps. Or perhaps his aim was to send a message to the Prussian government by criticizing political developments in a foreign country, using this indirect means to call for the full implementation of the reforms and transformations begun after Jena but now increasingly stalled. The history of Frederick William III's domestic politics, with his waverings, half-measures, abortive undertakings, both reactionary and progressive, would favor the latter hypothesis, which finds further confirmation of a sort from the fact that the publication of the third part of the article was halted by order of the king under the pretext that it constituted improper interference in another country's internal affairs. But whichever alternative one opts for, the critique of the English constitution contained in this article allows us to draw conclusions about what Hegel thought about conditions in Prussia.

Hegel states that England is historically backward because property is not fully transferable there, the State has not created a professional civil service, the law has not been codified and remains the secret possession of a corporation, and the crown is too weak to carry out the needed institutional transformation without resistance and violence.[20] On the Continent, he continues, the desired reforms that the

---

(Leipzig, 1920–23), vol. 4, *Die Germanische Welt,* 907, which describes how Hegel envisages Germany's role: "Its destiny being entirely spiritual, Germany has proved unable to achieve political unity . . . In terms of its international standing, Germany is a nullity." Hegel did not understand freedom in the same way that the "nationalists" did.

19. *Schriften zur Politik und Rechtsphilosophie,* 285.

20. It is curious to note that Hegel's critique, which remained unknown in England, covers all the points that were addressed by the reforms carried out over the course of the nineteenth century except those concerning the augmentation of

English are slowly groping toward have long since been carried out; in other words, Prussia is for him the model of perfect freedom, at least in regard to its principles. It is the State based on thought [*L'Etat de la pensée*], the State in which property is transferable and which possesses an administrative apparatus answerable to no one but the law, the State of Laws. In 1830 as in 1818 Hegel considers Prussia to be the modern State par excellence (which seems justified from the point of view of the historian), and he sees it in this way because he perceives it to be grounded in freedom.

At this point we can ask our question in a different form and even more insistently: How could Hegel see Prussia in this light? How could he oppose all the aspirations of "liberalism," nationalism, democracy, the whole range of nineteenth-century leftist ideology that to a large degree still constitutes the ideology of our own time and is one of the basic sources for all the propaganda to which we are currently subjected? And are we not telling only half of the story by simply recording his opposition to it? After all, did he not call on the State and the police to take action against the revolutionary movements of his day? Did he not denounce the ideologues who he thought were poisoning the minds of the young? Did he not inflame the cabinet to move against philosophical, theological, and political doctrines that he thought were endangering the State in its present form?[21]

Hegel could easily be excused for reacting in this way. Like all serious observers, he registered the failure of the French Revolution as it ran the course from terror to dictatorship to final defeat. In addition

---

royal power (instead of the king it was the prime minister who had the power of decision in Hegel's sense) (see vol. 3 of Elie Halévy, *A History of the English People in the Nineteenth Century,* trans. E. I. Watkin and D. A. Barker [New York, 1961]; or, among the numerous histories of the English constitution, the useful handbook by Thomas Pitt Taswell-Langmead, *English Constitutional History,* 10th ed., rev. Th. Plucknett [London, 1946]).

21. Accounts of Hegel's public interventions can be found in Haym, *Hegel und seine Zeit,* and Lenz, *Geschichte der Universität Berlin;* the positions of his defenders in Rosenkranz, *Apologie Hegels gegen R. Haym.*

(as I have already said), the events that were taking place as Hegel was writing the *Philosophy of Right*—the abortive revolutions of Italy and Spain as well as a spate of senseless political assassinations—only served to reinforce his mistrust of "direct action." Observation had shown him that lasting progress toward a freer society had only been achieved in the one State where it had been imposed from above by a group of remarkable civil servants, who, under royal protection, had been given the chance to operate without constraint, whereas both the established aristocracy in England and the revolutionary parties in the Latin countries were still facing, or facing once again, problems for which the solutions, if they had not yet been fully implemented, were rapidly on their way to being crowned with success in the State whose servant Hegel had just become.

But historical context is not the real issue. In philosophy the meaning of epithets such as *liberal, conservative,* or *reactionary* cannot be defined with any precision, and they only acquire such meaning as the end result of philosophical inquiry itself once, and to the degree that, it has managed to define what is meant by progress and determined the fundamental direction of history. To be sure, one can look at what has actually happened since then and say that history has proven Hegel wrong. But does this not throw us into a vicious circle? Is it not inconsistent to portray Hegel as the philosopher of the same Prussian state that threatened—and more than threatened—the whole of Europe for more than a century and then claim in the same breath that events have contradicted him? What is more, with this claim goes the assumption that history has issued its final judgment concerning the validity of the Hegelian conception of the State. Yet history never decides anything definitively—regression and "re-barbarization" will always remain a possibility—and if Prussia has now been "left behind" by history, which is now more than a probability, it would in fact prove Hegel correct in and for his time. Even if we ignore this objection, this does not mean that we have shown Hegel's conception of the State to be wrong. To do that it would be necessary to prove that it can only be applied to the Prussian State and no other.

In conclusion, there is only one way to proceed: to examine the *Philosophy of Right,* which for the fifteen years following Hegel's death was barely criticized, no more than it was during the lifetime of the author, only to then become, after 1848, the favorite target for all those who set out to "wreck" the Hegelian system.

## Chapter Two

# The Philosophical Foundations of Politics

It is common knowledge that the *Philosophy of Right* is full of "horrors." Here are some samples: the State is God on earth; society is subordinate to the State; our moral existence is less valuable than our political existence; the perfect form of the constitution is the monarchy; the people must obey the government; the idea of the nation is of no importance; loyalty toward the State is man's highest duty, indeed he *must* be a citizen;[1] an elected legislature is a bad system . . . and I shall omit the rest so as to get to the most horrific of them all, the famous line from the preface, so blasphemous that it has made all right-thinking men and women from every point along the political spectrum tremble with rage for more than a century: "What is rational is real, and what is real is rational" (*PhR* xix; Knox, 10).[2] What other re-

1. [The French reads: "la loyauté envers l'Etat est le devoir suprême de l'homme qui *doit* être citoyen," playing on the double meaning of *devoir* as noun, "duty," and verb, "to have to," so that obligation and necessity become confusingly interchangeable. TRANS.]

2. "Was vernünftig ist, das ist wirklich; und was wirklich ist, das ist vernünftig." The original text of the most significant quotations is provided in the notes because no translation can give the exact meaning of the original. To do this would require adhering to an accurate set of conventional French equivalents specially created to translate Hegelian terminology, which is not attempted here. The italics are Hegel's. [Weil's translation of the *Philosophy of Right* is given here. Hereafter it will be cited in the text as *PhR,* followed by the section number and page number from the 1821 German edition and then the page from the English translation by T. M. Knox (Oxford, 1953), the most widely used by English speakers. In this translation when Weil cites a German term in the body of his text it is given in parentheses,

action can there be to this thought except to say that it is a slap in the face of basic common sense, the final unforgivable insult, an outrage so shocking that most critics — at least this is the impression one gets from their works — find themselves unable to go any further, if not in their reading, at least in their understanding of the *Philosophy of Right?*

Yet Hegel took great pains to explain what he meant by this sentence. As he pointed out,[3] one had only to open his *Logic* to see that in his terminology *reality* and *existence* are not the same at all,[4] since existence was only partially equivalent to reality, the remainder being made up by *appearance*. His efforts were in vain. Haym, for example, declares that it is precisely this distinction that is to blame for the entire system's fundamental weakness because it lets Hegel limit his philosophy of the State to the confines of simple empirical reality.[5] This is how Haym sees the matter, but how can any system, at least that part of it dealing with moral and political issues (i.e., the very areas where it must treat the topic of action), abandon the distinction between the real and the apparent, the significant and the insignificant, or the essential and the inessential?

It is incumbent on Hegel's critics, then, to show that he has put the emphasis in the wrong place and asserted that something was *real* when it was only *existent*. Is this the case? Haym, an intelligent

---

and when he cites a German term in his quotations of Hegel it is given in square brackets. TRANS.]

3. *Encyclopedia,* ed. G. Lasson, 3d ed. (Leipzig, 1923), §6. Moreover, *PhR* itself precisely defines the difference (§1, 3; Knox, 14).

4. The German word I have translated as "reality" is *Wirklichkeit,* from *wirken,* meaning "act by creating" or "to produce an effect on reality," whereas the French word refers through *res* to the object as it is experienced, a passive, theoretical object. If I were being faithful to etymology, I would have translated what Hegel calls *Dasein* as "reality" instead of as "existence" (giving the terms *Dasein* and *existence* a meaning quite different from that given them by Heidegger and the existentialists). It is impossible to translate the words *Wirklichkeit* and *Dasein* in such a way that they continue to exhibit their etymological derivation while also retaining the whole range of their potential usage in German. Thus, my translation must be even more reliant on the etymological interconnections specific to the French lexicon, its *harmonics* if you will, which are completely different from those of German.

5. Haym, *Hegel und seine Zeit,* 368.

critic, did not miss the opportunity of stating his difference from Hegel in the clearest possible terms: Hegel is prepared to sacrifice the individual because the interests of harmony must outweigh those of concrete, living individuality.[6] Hegel's response would be (and in fact was) to ask, Can individuality be rational in itself? Is not the rational necessarily the universal? Can individuality desire anything more than to be reconciled with the reality of the rational, to discover itself in what *is* insofar as it is rational? And then again, if we take Haym's critique seriously, does it not apply to any philosophy whatsoever?

It is telling that Haym could find this very argument, phrased somewhat differently, in the same preface to the *Philosophy of Right,* the main source for his critique:

> As far as nature is concerned, it is granted that philosophy has to know it as it is, that the philosopher's stone is hidden somewhere, but hidden in nature itself, that nature is rational in itself, and that knowledge has to investigate and grasp through the understanding this reason that is present and actual in it [i.e., nature]; [that what must be grasped by reason is] not the formations and accidents, which can be observed on the surface, but nature's eternal harmony, and this in the sense of the law and essence *immanent* within it. On the other hand, it is said that the ethical [*sittlich*] world, the State, reason as it realizes itself in the element of self-consciousness, does not enjoy this good fortune [which consists in] its being reason that has achieved power and mastery within that element and maintains itself and has its home there. No, it is said that the universe of spirit is at the mercy of chance and caprice, forsaken by God, with the result that if one accepts this atheism of the ethical world, Truth only exists outside of it, and that at the same time, because reason is *also* supposed to be in it, Truth is nothing but a problem there. (*PhR* ix; Knox, 4)[7]

6. Ibid., 369 ff.

7. "Von der *Natur* gibt man zu, daß die Philosophie sie zu erkennen habe, *wie sie ist,* daß der Stein der Weisen *irgendwo,* aber in der Natur *selbst* verborgen liege, daß

Hegel draws a striking parallel here between nature and politics. He refuses to accept that reason can only be discovered in natural phenomena, while the domain of action and history must be abandoned to feeling, desire, and passion. Just as there is a science of nature, there is a science of the State, and reason is no harder to discern in the productions of human consciousness than it is in natural phenomena (whose intelligibility, their essential rationality, is readily accepted as being easily comprehensible to everyone). The ethical world *really exists,* and to an infinitely higher degree than nature, which is pure exteriority.

> On the one hand, the relationship that the ethical [*sittlich*] substance, its laws, and its powers, as objects, have with the subject is that they *are,* in the highest sense of being autonomous— an absolute authority and power infinitely more solid than the being of nature . . . The authority of ethical laws is infinitely higher because natural objects only represent reason [*Vernünftigkeit*] in an external and isolated manner and hide it under the form of chance. (*PhR* §146, 157; Knox, 105–6) [8]

In order to obviate the common misunderstanding that sees strong evidence in this passage to support the charges of absolutism or rela-

---

sie *in sich vernünftig* sei und das Wissen diese in ihr gegenwärtige, *wirkliche* Vernunft, nicht die auf der Oberfläche sich zeigenden Gestaltungen und Zufälligkeiten, sondern ihre ewige Harmonie, aber als ihr *immanentes* Gesetz und Wesen zu erforschen und begreifend zu fassen habe. Die *sittliche Welt* dagegen, der Staat, sie, die vernunft, wie sie sich im Elemente des Selbstbewußtseins verwirklicht, soll nicht des Glücks genießen, daß es die Vernunft ist, welche in der Tat in diesem Elemente sich zur Kraft und Gewalt gebracht habe, darin behaupte und inwohne. Das geistige Universum soll vielmehr dem Zufall und der Willkür preisgegeben, es soll *gottverlassen* sein, so daß nach diesem Atheismus der sittlichen Welt das *Wahre* sich *außer* ihr befinde, und zugleich, weil doch *auch* Vernunft darin sein soll, das Wahre nur ein Problema sei."

8. "Für das Subjekt haben die sittliche Substanz, ihre Gesetze und Gewalten einerseits als Gegenstand das Verhältnis, daß sie *sind,* im höchsten Sinne der Selbständigkeit,—eine absolute, unendlich festere Autorität und Macht als das Sein der Natur . . . Die Autorität der sittlichen Gesetze ist unendlich höher, weil die Naturdinge nur auf die ganz *äußerliche* und *vereinzelte* Weise die Vernünftigkeit darstellen und sie unter die Gestalt der Zufälligkeit verbergen."

tivism traditionally leveled against Hegel (because it is taken as read that in his theory the State completes and supersedes [*achève*] the realm of morality, but there is no agreement about whether we should then infer that he was a rigorous statist or a moral relativist), we need do no more than look at what appears on the "other hand" of the argument as presented in the following paragraph:

> For the subject, on the other hand, they [ethical powers] are not something alien, but through the witness borne by the spirit he [the subject] affirms them to be his own essence, the essence in which he has his feeling of himself, and in which he lives as in his own element indistinguishable from himself. (*PhR* §147, 158; Knox, 106)[9]

Man's life is rational, and he knows this to be the case, even though what I am referring to as knowledge might be limited (and will remain so for some time) to the knowledge afforded him from the feeling that he enjoys an immediate relation to the moral world.

If my main concern were Hegelian ontology or the ontological foundations of his political theory, I would underline the fact that the use of the concepts of *feeling* and *immediate knowledge* (this term can be found in a phrase following the passage quoted above) demonstrates in and of itself that the passage from the ethical world and feeling to the State is a necessary one. But something else is important here, namely, the affirmation that the world in which people live, in which they know themselves to be at home (because even their dissatisfactions only have meaning in relation to this world), is rational and that the laws that govern our lives can be known, and can be known in the deepest sense of the word, since it is in them that reason not only realizes itself [*se réalise*][10] (it realizes itself everywhere

9. "Andererseits sind sie dem Subjekte nicht ein *Fremdes*, sondern es gibt das *Zeugnis des Geistes* von ihnen als *von seinem eigenen Wesen*, in welchem es sein *Selbstgefühl* hat, und darin als seinem von sich ununterschiedenen Elemente lebt."

10. [The verb *réaliser* is translated as "realize" throughout. This apparent distortion relies on both senses of the word in English, the more common "to be or become aware of something" and the primary but less common meaning, "to bring into concrete existence" (*Webster's Collegiate Dictionary*, 10th ed.), which has remained the

else as well) but, more than that, will ultimately come to *know* that it has realized itself. The theory of the State, of the State *as it really is,* not the State of utopian dreamers, is therefore the theory of reason as it is realized in man, realized *for* itself and *by* itself.

It is not a desire for, but a theory of and a search [*recherche*] for, the State: the good State can be sought [*chercher*] [11] because *there is* a State. But what we are searching for [*cherche*] under the name of the good State is never anything but the State *tout court* as it is in itself for reason. What is more, this search cannot be anything other than a theoretical one, in other words, a search for that which is real, because science—and we are in the domain of science here—deals with what is really there: "philosophy is its own time grasped in thought" (*PhR* xxi–xxii; Knox, 11).[12] Despite which, Hegel adds, if we listened to those who call for or propose new and original theories of the State, one would think

> that there had never yet been any State or State constitution in the world and that none existed at the present time, but that we must rather begin at the beginning *now*—and this "now" goes on forever—and that the ethical world had always been wait- ing for us to proceed only *now* to the elaboration, analysis, and construction of foundations. (*PhR* ix; Knox, 4)[13]

But nothing is more absurd than to expect philosophy to provide recipes or lessons on how the world ought to be made. On the con-

---

basic meaning in French and whose double sense best captures the Hegelian dia- lectical movement in which knowledge grows out of being and self-actualization rather than being opposed to them. The potentially passive sense of *se réaliser* adds to the fullest expression of this fusion of subject and object. TRANS.]

11. [There is an untranslatable play on the words *recherche* and *chercher* here: *recher- che* means "a search for" but also "research," intellectual investigation in the academic sense, and *chercher* means primarily "to look, search for" but also forms the root of *recherche*. TRANS.]

12. "So ist auch die Philosophie, *ihre Zeit in Gedanken erfaßt.*"

13. "[S]o sollte man meinen, als ob noch kein Staat und Staatsverfassung in der Welt gewesen, noch gegenwärtig vorhanden sei, sondern als ob man *jetzt*—und dies *Jetzt* dauert immer fort—ganz von vorne anzufangen, und die sittliche Welt nur auf ein solches jetziges Ausdenken und Ergründen und Begründen gewartet habe."

trary, "as the thought of the world, it appears only when reality has completed its process of formation and reached a finished state" (*PhR* xxiv; Knox, 12–13).[14]

There can be knowledge of the State as it is in itself, which is knowledge of an *idea* of the State. But this idea differs from the Platonic idea of the State in that it is historical: it is not an idea that exists outside of becoming [*devenir*][15] but an idea bound up with becoming itself,[16] at the same time remaining an objective knowledge that does not have to take feelings, opinions, or desires into account except insofar as these feelings lead to action and shape reality, a knowledge that does not have to take a partisan position except in favor of the truth.

It is evident from the passages we referred to above[17] that this notion of the State does not and cannot possibly mean that each and every State is a perfect State, that any State is *right* [*a raison*][18] in everything that it does, and that the individual is obliged to give it unquestioning obedience. In fact, they furnish convincing proof that if the law is reality in the strongest sense, it is also the reality least foreign to man. Hegel's philosophy interprets the whole of history in the same way: as the reconciliation of the individual with the universal. However, since the majority of the attacks on Hegel accusing him of conformism are directed precisely at this principle, it will be helpful to look

14. "Als der *Gedanke* der Welt erscheint sie erst in der Zeit, nachdem die Wirklichkeit ihren Bildungsprozeß vollendet und sich fertig gemacht hat."

15. [The French word *devenir*, here translated as "becoming," is the standard translation of Hegel's logical and metaphysical term *Das Werden*, but it can also mean "development" and is translated as such when appropriate. TRANS.]

16. This "idea" is therefore normative in the sense that it gives us the possibility of evaluating [*apprécier*] everything that exists. But in another sense it is not normative, and this is the crucial point: it does not furnish us with a timeless or extratemporal model. See below, the role of history.

17. See above, nn. 8 and 9.

18. [In French the phrase reads, "que n'importe quel Etat ait *raison* en tout ce qu'il fait." Weil italicizes *raison* to bring out the double sense of *avoir raison*, which in French means "to be right" but in the present context also means "to possess reason," i.e., to be rational. TRANS.]

at some other texts that demonstrate that he was able to draw the proper consequences from it.

> When we are referring to the idea of the State, we must not represent particular States or particular institutions to ourselves. Instead we must consider the idea, this real [*wirklich*] God existing by itself [*für sich*]. Any State, even if it can be declared to be bad according to a given principle held by someone or other, and even if such a defect may be found in it, any State, especially if it can be counted among the developed States of our time, bears all the essential moments of the State's existence in itself. But since it is easier to find defects than to understand the positive side of things, we all too easily make the mistake of focusing on its isolated aspects and thus forget about the organic nature[19] of the State. The State is not a work of art; it functions in the world and thus in the sphere of caprice, chance, and error, and bad behavior may disfigure it in many respects. But the ugliest of men, the criminal, the invalid, or the cripple, are still living human beings. Life, the positive, persists in them despite their defects, and it is this positive factor that is our theme here. (*PhR* add. to §258; Knox, 279)[20]

19. [Hegel uses the expression "Inwendigen Organismus." TRANS.]

20. "Bei der Idee des Staates muß man nicht besondere Staaten vor Augen haben, nicht besondere Institutionen, man muß vielmehr die Idee, diesen wirklichen Gott, für sich betrachten. Jeder Staat, man mag ihn auch nach den Grundsätzen, die man hat, für schlecht erklären, man mag diese oder jene Mangelhaftigkeit daran erkennen, hat immer, wenn er namentlich zu den ausgebildeten unserer Zeit gehört, die wesentliche Momente seiner Existenz in sich. Weil es aber leichter ist Mängel aufzufinden, als das Affirmative zu begreifen, verfällt man leicht in den Fehler, über einzelne Seiten den inwendigen Organismus des Staates selbst zu vergessen. Der Staat ist kein Kunstwerk; er steht in der Welt, somit in der Sphäre der Willkür, des Zufalls und des Irrtums, übles Benehmen kann ihn nach vielen Seiten defigurieren. Aber der häßlichste Mensch, der Verbrecher, ein Kranker und Krüppel ist immer noch ein lebender Mensch; das Affirmative, das Leben, besteht trotz des Mangels, und um dieses Affirmative ist es hier zu tun." This is one of the additions that the first editors of the *Complete Works* took from Hegel's lectures. It is used here because the texts I cite below corroborate that the expression used here is in complete agreement with Hegel's published opinions.

The turn inward (Hegel is referring to the individual who turns away from the State, in particular Socrates, who opposed the principle of moral consciousness to the Athenian State) occurs

> in ages when what is recognized as right and good in contemporary reality and tradition [Sitte] cannot satisfy the best will; when the existing world of freedom has become faithless to it [the best will], it can no longer find itself in the duties still expected of it. (PhR §138, 134–35; Knox, 92) [21]

A norm of the law can be deductively proven to be well grounded in and consistent with existing conditions and institutions and yet can be contrary to the law and irrational in and for itself. (PhR §3, 8; Knox, 17) [22]

The positive science of law should not be astonished when it is asked if . . . a norm of the law is also rational. (PhR §212, 211; Knox, 136) [23]

The fact that historically speaking there have been barbarous ages and conditions when everything belonging to the higher forms of spirit was nurtured in the Church, when the State was only a worldly regime of violence, caprice, and passion . . . belongs to history [and has therefore happened once and can happen again]. (PhR §270, 267–68; Knox, 171) [24]

21. "[I]n Epochen, wo das, was als das Rechte und Gute in der Wirklichkeit und Sitte gilt, den besseren Willen nicht befriedigen kann; wenn die vorhandene Welt der Freiheit ihm ungetreu geworden, findet er sich in den geltenden Pflichten nicht mehr."

22. "Eine Rechtsbestimmung kann sich aus den *Umständen* und *vorhandenen* Rechts-Institutionen als vollkommen *gegründet* und *konsequent* zeigen lassen und doch an und für sich unrechtlich und unvernünftig sein." See also §30.

23. "Die positive Rechtswissenschaft . . . darf . . . sich wenigstens nicht absolut verwundern, wenn sie es auch als eine *Querfrage* für ihre Beschäftigung ansieht, wenn nun gefragt wird, ob denn nach allen diesen Beweisen eine rechtsbestimmung *vernünftig* ist."

24. "Daß es nun geschichtlich Zeiten und Zustände von Barbarei gegeben, wo alles höhere Geistige in der Kirche seinen Sitz hatte und der Staat nur ein weltliches

What is common to all these passages—one could easily find more —is the insistence on according men the right to criticize and oppose the State. Hegel does not doubt that the empirical State can be imperfect, that everything is not always for the best in the best of all possible worlds, that positive law can be irrational, and that real States can be left behind in the wake of history. This does not alter the simple fact that nothing of any value can be said before one knows that whereof one speaks, that one cannot judge *States* before knowing what *the State* is.

\* \* \*

There is nothing to prevent someone from asserting that this entire discussion is meaningless, that there is no such thing as the State in itself, that the idea of political philosophy is absurd, that we should simply live and let live, that one person's opinion is as good as another's, and that when all is said and done success is the ultimate judge, not of theories—there are no longer *any* theories at this point in the argument—but of the fate of individuals who rely on so-called theories. In short, there is nothing to prevent us from saying that there is no such thing as history, only a series of events devoid of meaning because they are devoid of any structure capable of giving them cohesion and unity.[25] Nothing to prevent us, indeed, but it fol-

---

Regiment der Gewalttätigkeit, der Willkür und Leidenschaft und jener abstrakte Gegensatz das Hauptprinzip der Wirklichkeit war, gehört in die Geschichte."

[The penultimate clause, omitted by Weil, can be translated "and that abstract opposition was the fundamental principle of reality." TRANS.]

25. This theory is often attributed to Hegel himself, suggesting that the Hegelian conception of history would vindicate whoever wins the struggle and that it would then be the victor's "idea" that prevailed. It is clear that his entire theory of the State is opposed to such an interpretation. However, it is plausible for two reasons: in the struggle for recognition preceding the foundation of the State it is the result of the struggle that is decisive (see the *Phenomenology of Spirit* and the commentary by A. Kojève, *Introduction to the Reading of Hegel,* trans. James H. Nichols [New York, 1969], esp. 3 ff.). Not only is it not a question of a struggle within the State (which arises only out of the struggle for recognition) but the progress of Spirit is the work not of the victor but of the vanquished, of the slave. It is true that as Hegel de-

lows from this that whoever appeals to violence as the unique cause of events has thereby lost the right to protest against it. Certainly, we can observe—and Plato was only the first to do so—that the supporters of violence in theory defend strict morality as soon as they themselves become victims of violence, that those who habitually resort to violence turn around at the first sign of imminent defeat and appeal to the tribunal of destiny or divinity, the meaning of History, or venerable rules predating all our positive norms and are the first to complain if some organized body, that is to say, the State, no longer operates to their satisfaction. However, since it is quite respectable nowadays to champion a social atomism that recognizes no other social entity but the individual, let us play devil's advocate and suppose that men were to subscribe to the principle of atomism and acknowledge nothing except their individual wills (called "arbitrary" by philosophers). How far does its acceptance limit the possibility of producing a theory of the State?

Not at all, says Hegel. On the contrary, the individualist position expresses an essential aspect of human life, a *moment* without which any understanding of the State itself would be impossible, an essential moment but a subordinate one. It is well known—although we will have to come back to this later—that for Hegel right [*le droit*] precedes morality, formal morality precedes the concrete ethics of communal life (the living tradition he terms *Sittlichkeit*),[26] and the latter precedes the State, which is in turn its reality *(Wirklichkeit)* and its total fulfillment. But the immediate significance of this ascending sequence is that the individual's right and morality are therefore imprescriptible,

---

scribes it, history is made by the violent exploits of a *hero,* on the one hand, and by war between sovereign States, on the other, and that the State is dependent on both types of action, whether for its foundation or transformation or for its rise to supremacy. But foundation and victory only take on positive value in Hegel's theory when they bring about further progress toward the realization of freedom, that is, in Hegelian terms, reason. See my remarks below on the hero and history.

26. [I have followed the English convention of translating the concept Hegel expresses by *Moralität* as "morality" and *Sittlichkeit* as "ethics," although here the French reads, "la morale formelle . . . la morale concrète" and generally does not differentiate by lexical change. TRANS.]

and although at a more developed level the theory signifies that they are insufficient in themselves, ultimately it signifies that their reality —and not their destruction—can only be sought in the State. This does not mean that the State can or should suppress or challenge the right and morality of the human person. Quite the reverse. As always with Hegel, whatever is suppressed dialectically is also sublimated and preserved and is in fact only fully realized by this act of *Aufheben*.

At this point the fundamental problem to consider becomes that of freedom or, what amounts to the same thing, will. Politics—in its broadest sense, as encompassing the whole science of the common life shared by the political animal known as a man, that is, law, morality, tradition, the organization of both society and the State—is nothing but the science of the will.[27] Man *finds* himself in the world; he finds himself there in the same way that he finds anything else, as something given. Strictly speaking, he can not even be said to *find* himself at first because he is not yet opposed to himself. He exists, and his way of being is to be conscious of the outside world, not of himself. It is only at the moment when he begins to *reflect in himself* [*se réfléter en lui-même*], to use Hegel's intriguing expression, when he is thrown back on himself, that the will no longer simply *is* but manifests itself in and to man as man himself [*l'homme même*]. He becomes conscious of himself thanks to the failure and defeat he suffers when he struggles with another will and does not succeed in dominating it.[28] By showing itself to man in this way, the will reveals itself to him as thought.[29] Nothing is more surprising at first glance nor more obvious on reflection: the will that is mine, that I know to be mine, is the *thought* of the negation of all and any condition; it is the *thought* of my freedom, the *thought* that I can refuse the given. But in refusing all given, and all external (natural condition, need, etc.) or internal (desire, inclination, instinct, etc.) determination, by becoming conscious of myself as free negativity and a freedom that negates, I simultaneously discover

27. For what follows see *PhR*, §§4 ff.
28. See Kojève, *Introduction to the Reading of Hegel*.
29. *PhR* §§5 ff.

a new positivity just as essential as this negativity: I deny in order to posit, I am absolute freedom insofar as I can choose something in particular; I reject *one thing* in order to choose *another,* continuing to want it until I choose something else, always certain that I can deny whatever I have just posited, but also deciding what I am in and by this new act of freedom. Freedom—as everyone has recently been declaring, as if they had just made an amazing discovery and finally stumbled on a philosophical panacea—is freedom "in situation." [30]

30. There is nothing new about the idea of *freedom "in situation."* The concept is as old as philosophy itself. It was never expressed as such for the simple reason that before Kant's denial of the empirical world's significance—a denial based on his espousal of transcendental morality [*l'acosmisme sur fond moral*]—no one had ever imagined that freedom could possibly exist outside a concrete situation. The glory of rediscovery (or if one prefers, the discovery, to reserve the merit of discovery itself for the fully elaborated formulation of a thesis whose basic content had long been accepted) belongs to Hegel, who understood both the importance of this idea and its inadequacy (see below, the discussion on Kant and Rousseau). In rediscoveries made more recently we can discern a return to the Kantian attitude (although it cannot be said that current work in this vein always attains either the depth or the sublimity of Kant's thought) coupled with the *requirement* of meaning in life, of a moral cosmos whose *realization* or *reality* is nevertheless considered to be impossible in any philosophically legitimate or legitimizable manner. Once this point was reached, self-consistency would have required the next step to extend agnosticism much further than did Kant, for whom the words *God, freedom,* and *immortality* still had a meaning, even though it was no longer permissible to articulate it within the limits of his theory.

If "man is a useless passion" (J.-P. Sartre, *Being and Nothingness,* trans. Hazel Barnes [New York, 1956], 524)—a definition that is equivalent to the one Hegel gives of the *person* in private law and does not go beyond it—then philosophy can no longer understand its own possibility and must eventuate in either poetry or the *acte gratuit,* that is, in *wild* speech and action. In fact men know very well what matters in their lives, and even their doubts can always be clearly articulated because their concrete existence confronts them with questions, which they answer. (That the answers they give are sometimes good and sometimes bad is in itself proof that life has a meaning, which does not mean that it is easily discovered.) Moreover, the source of this new *philosophy of reflection,* which separates man from reason, M. Heidegger, aptly remarks that concrete human life takes place in the mode of *Zuhandenheit,* in a world that is well known and familiar and only becomes problematic in exceptional cases, one in which men are so comfortably placed in situation that normally they do not feel themselves to be in situation (*Being and Time,* trans. John Macquarrie and Edward Robinson [New York, 1962], §16, 102 ff.). It would be instructive to find

In other words, because the will is *free* it *necessarily* gives itself a content, a goal that must be realized, in reality and using means furnished by reality. In its original form freedom of the will is the will to realize a goal, and nothing more. This is not to deny that freedom and self-consciousness are already co-present with the will, but neither of them is apprehended as such; man wills freely, his consciousness is self-consciousness, but in everyday life he remains unaware of this. He is not interested in anything except the immediate world he sees before him—it is we philosophers who have proclaimed that man has attained a level of development superior to that of animal kingdom. He is free *in himself* [*en soi*] for us [*pour nous*], the philosophers, not *for himself* [*pour soi*]. He has *certainty* of his freedom but no knowledge of it.

---

out how and why this real world gets transformed into an inauthentic world, how and why an *authentic existence* detaches itself from everyday existence and, although it is not necessarily accorded a higher value in comparison (in Heidegger there is no *preference* for one or the other of these attitudes), nevertheless becomes the center of interest. Hegel gave a brief account of what a philosophy of formal existence and decision (which he still called virtue) might look like, only to reject it:

When they are discoursing about virtue *in general,* people easily run the risk of mouthing pompous platitudes because they are discoursing about something abstract and indeterminate; conversely, such a discourse, with its reasons and images, addresses itself to the individual understood as caprice and subjective pleasure-seeking. In any given ethical order in which a system of ethical relations has been fully developed and realized, virtue, in the strict sense of the word, only has its place and effective reality in exceptional circumstances and when exceptional conflicts arise in social relations—in genuine conflicts, that is, since moral reflection can fabricate conflicts all over the place and furnish itself the consciousness of being in special circumstances and of having made sacrifices.

[Das Reden aber von der Tugend grenzt leicht an leere Deklamation, weil damit nur von einem Abstrakten und Unbestimmten gesprochen wird, sowie auch solche Rede mit ihren Gründen und Darstellungen sich an das Individuum als an eine Willkür und subjektives Belieben wendet. Unter einem vorhandenen sittlichen Zustande, dessen Verhältnisse vollständig entwickelt und verwirklicht sind, hat die *eigentliche Tugend* nur in außerordentlichen Umständen und Kollisionen jener Verhältnisse ihre Stelle und Wirklichkeit;—in wahrhaften *Kollisionen,* denn die moralische Reflexion kann sich allenthalben Kollisionen erschaffen und sich das Bewußtsein von etwas Besonderem und von gebrachten Opfern geben.]

(*PhR* §150, 161; Knox, 107–8).

"Normal" consciousness cannot go beyond this point since it is—and is nothing more than—this certainty of being able to negate any given, oppose any limitation, and refuse whatever is imposed [*imposé*] or merely offered [*posé*] to it from outside. This explains why the expressions *rational* and *universal will* arouse such intense opposition as soon as they are used. But those who react in this way have forgotten the positive correlate indissolubly attached to this negativity. Will always has a content, and as long as this content itself is not determined by the will, as long as it is decided by chance factors such as blind preference, taste, or personal characteristics, that is, as long as it is *arbitrary,* that version of determinism is true that claims that negativity does not function in any other context except that of a concrete situation and that the situation as well as an individual's "reactions" to it are both already given. So that whereas the fact that I choose depends on my freedom, *how* I choose—the only thing that really matters—depends on causality.

For Hegel the partial truth of determinism is based on the fact that the individual will, and here I am speaking of its own self-conception, is properly speaking not yet a human will since it seeks to obtain its goal *immediately* and is therefore not *mediated* by an active reason, by the conscious organization of a life in common—in short, because (like everything that is unmediated) it is *natural*. A further step must be taken for the will to grasp itself as a will that does more than simply will, but *wills freedom*. It is only by giving itself its own content that the will achieves freedom, for the content of a will that is free and independent of any given can only be freedom itself.

This is a paradoxical and apparently incomprehensible affirmation. How can free will will freedom, positively will negativity? It can do so because it is not willing the absolute and naked negativity of an already given and unfree individuality. It has come to understand that negativity denies everything given as such, everything unmediated by human action, including the empirical being of individuals themselves, everything that does not satisfy *reason*. We shall see later that negativity is not discarded as a result of this new understanding and that it continues to play a decisive role at the level of both individual and social life. However, once will attains the realm of *thought,* it has in effect returned to itself and now understands itself as being in essence nonarbitrary. What it previously had willed without understanding that it was willing it, it can henceforth recognize as the work and product of its own creative activity. We shall see in an analogous case below *how* freedom's coming to consciousness is elaborated in the progressive transition from right to morality, thence to concrete ethical life, and finally to the State. What is important here is the thesis that free will can only fulfill itself when it comes to understand that it seeks, and has always sought, freedom in a rational and universal *organization* of freedom (with the genitive taken in the subjective as well the objective sense). The *will* that is free not only for us, not only for itself, but in *and* for itself, this will is equally *thought* realizing itself, knowing that it realizes itself and that it has already realized itself.[31]

Whatever the time or the place, we must not lose sight of the fact

31. The important question to ask at this point, namely, whether this realization of freedom is complete, in other words, whether history, which is the realization of freedom, is over and done with, will be taken up in the final section of this book. Let us note for now that what has already been said, including the passages quoted, allows us to formulate a preliminary response: in each historical instant in which thought is present, freedom is realized; otherwise there would be no thought. But the realization of freedom is not complete; otherwise history would not have continued. However, it is always complete relatively speaking; that is, at each stage it corresponds to the consciousness of the age, just as thought corresponds to the reality of the age. The next step forward in history will be taken not by those who are representative of the thought of their age but by those who are unsatisfied, those who are driven to act by passion. The charge of "historicism" often leveled at Hegel is therefore unjustified. History possesses a determinate meaning because its end is the realization of freedom-reason, the organization of life lived in common, in which every individual will find satisfaction insofar as he is rational (by the suppression of all unmediated and inhuman relations with nature). Whatever has been acquired in the process is retained, and any attempt to turn back is, strictly speaking, irrational and therefore immoral. (Although it is well known that such attempts can be made and that there is nothing to prevent them from succeeding— the sole consequence of which is that history has to do its work over again.) As for the morality of the individual, it is concretely determined by the tradition (*Sitte*) of his people and his time. Not to conform to it would be criminal unless the individual's action becomes universal and so expresses a new consciousness that must justify itself historically *and* morally—which amounts to the same thing.

that politics is the science of the rational will in its effective reality *(Wirklichkeit)*, the science of the historical realization of freedom, of the positive realization of negativity. Freedom is only positive and effective insofar as it is objectively—whether consciously or not— rational, that is, universal. It is conceptually and practically impossible for concrete freedom to be brought about by the arbitrary decision of the *individual*. Rather, man is free only insofar as he wants the freedom of *man* in a free community.[32]

*   *   *

This conclusion allows us to understand why Hegel's discussion of freedom starts out not with a "metaphysical" disquisition but with an analysis of concrete freedom in its most primitive, simple, and abstract form, and yet the one in which it appears *objectively:* the form of right. Primitive right, the first objective expression of the will, is the empirical realization of the empirical and natural will of the individual. It is the right of the individual as such, the right to have *property,* which for Hegel is distinguished from *wealth,* from property that yields profit and guarantees the economic independence of an individual, family, or society. Property means the possession of a natural object. With this act natural men make themselves *persons.* It is not

32. For convincing evidence that the Hegelian thesis can be justified outside the "philosophical" realm—which for many relies on the almost exact opposite of a serious and scientific demonstration—it behooves us to study B. Malinowski's *Freedom and Civilization* (London, 1947). Malinowski begins with the presuppositions of his own particular discipline (ethnology) and repeats, despite or because of his profound disdain for "metaphysics" in general and Hegel in particular, the greater part of Hegel's theses. He never conflicts with Hegel, not even in those areas where he does not achieve equally profound or far-reaching results. This is especially true of his conception of freedom, by which both he and Hegel mean positive freedom, the freedom to do something, not *negative* freedom, the freedom not to do something, and which for Malinowski too can only be asserted of the constitution of a society, and not an individual consciousness, which is essentially arbitrary insofar as it is individual. The comparison could be extended to cover all aspects of his book. See the summary of Malinowski's book in *Critique* 4 (1947): 356 ff.

need that is at the origin of property; it is the affirmation of individuality, the act of will, constituting the person to such an extent that my body is me only insofar as I take possession of it (although for another person I am never anything else but my body). On the other hand, nothing that can be individualized is exempt from being taken possession of, nothing is protected from the right that I have to use it as I please, no limit can be drawn to the right of property at the level of abstract right, which is abstract precisely because of the absence of any limitation enforced by a superior positivity.[33]

But since it is my will that has deposited itself in a given object, it can just as easily withdraw from it, and just as it has alienated and externalized *(veräußern)* itself in the thing, it can alienate the thing in turn. This movement makes manifest the passage from individual right to contract to the formation of a common will between the parties to a contract, which nevertheless remains particular to them and does not attain universality. It is also clear that there is nothing to prevent this will from being perverted and that it is quite distinct from the will as it is in and for itself, the rational and universal will. It remains in the grip of its *other,* in what is external and given to it; it is therefore far from being free will according to its abstract definition "the free will which wills the free will" (*PhR* §27, 33–34; Knox, 32).[34]

In this way damages and crime fall under the aegis of right because it governs everything that is external, natural, and aleatory. Force and constraint have not been expunged from contract's incomplete expression of freedom. But since freedom, even in an alienated and external form, as it is here, cannot exist under any constraint, which is the contrary of personal right, force and constraint cancel themselves out. By denying the person of the other, the criminal has denied personhood itself and therefore his own. Since he is in essence rational, he has willed, in himself [*en soi*] if not for himself [*pour soi*], that right be reestablished by a counterconstraint. As a result, something that up to this point had been true in purely philosophical terms gets articu-

---

33. For what follows see *PhR,* pt. 1, "Abstract Right."
34. "Der freie Wille, der den freien Willen will."

lated in a more explicit fashion: the opposition between the universal
will, which exists exclusively as an object in itself [*en soi*], that is, for us
who proceed in this inquiry from the point of view of reason, the universal, and science, and the individual will, which is free exclusively
for itself [*pour elle-même*]. It is by means of damages (in civil cases)
and crime (governed by the penal code) that justice is revealed to be
the object of will in its deepest sense, which opposes the arbitrary to
freedom and alienation to reason. Man does not really will the evil he
does because he does not want evil to be done, given that evil annuls
not only rational freedom but even arbitrary freedom insofar as even
the arbitrary affirms not only the autonomy of this *particular* man but
the autonomy of *man* as such. For the person who has understood
injustice (it is not certain that every individual will attain such understanding, but it is not indispensable either) the person as legally defined can no longer be considered man in his totality. He understands
himself to be an individual will, but in his individual will he wants
to be universal; in Hegel's terminology, the *person* becomes a *subject*.

Both the person and the subject act, but the subject no longer ex-
ternalizes himself completely or naively in his act. He assigns the
goal of his action for himself and thus is conscious of it. What matters to him is that his will be in accord with itself and not fall into
self-contradiction or self-refutation. In other words, the will of the
subject wants to be a universal will and knows that it can only be so
if it conforms to the concept of reason. The *good will* is the human
will as such, and good action is determined through the fact that,
although it remains *my* action, it makes that concept its maxim which
tells it what it *ought* to be, so that as a will it will represent the will
of *all* men. With these notions we are now squarely in the domain of
Kant's moral theory.

*  *  *

The critique of the Kantian conception of morality that closes this
part of the *Philosophy of Right* has been a favorite topic of all those who
have written on Hegel. It recurs in a basically identical form in prac-

tically all of Hegel's works, from the *Difference between the Systems of Fichte and Schelling* to the final editions of the *Encyclopedia of the Philosophical Sciences.* The central thread of this critique is well known: the categorical imperative does not enable us to take any action because the concrete content necessary for application of the moral criterion must be taken from the existing world—the realm of the external and the arbitrary—whereas the moral criterion itself is purely formal. Thus in Kant duty remains forever pure duty, and, what is worse, it must remain pure because were the moral law ever to be followed by all men, they would no longer have any task or problem to tackle and thus would no longer have any content for their moral consciousness.

Be that as it may, in regard to the question that most concerns us, this critique, definitive though it is, is less relevant than the positive content of the part of the *Philosophy of Right* mentioned above, which explores the topic of action understood as action belonging to me and for which I bear and claim responsibility, whether it is good or bad, praiseworthy or culpable. This type of action is therefore the result of my deliberate resolution *(Vorsatz)* and taken with my own ends in mind. But since action is carried out in the world and exposed to the hazards of external reality, the will ultimately leaves the isolation of resolution behind for the universality of *intention (Absicht)*. The subject does not seek simply to accomplish a specific and separate act; he searches for himself in his acts. He does not pursue one object and then another ad infinitum; he pursues his satisfaction. This satisfaction is not tied to any isolated content, nor is it the satisfaction of a particular individual: it is the satisfaction of the *subject,* meaning man insofar as he is a thinking being. It is the satisfaction of the subjective, but in the objective, satisfaction in a *work* [*oeuvre*].[35] It will not be immoral because it is the satisfaction of a free being. Or more accurately, it *ought* not to be immoral but risks becoming so because the good of the subject, of subjects, of all men, has not yet been definitively ascertained.

35. [I have translated *oeuvre* as "work" and *travail* and its verbal forms as "labor." TRANS.]

That is, until now: the good is the unity of the particular will with the universal will. In other words, the good exists only as the *truth* (revealed being) of the will, therefore in thought and by thought, for only thought, and thought alone, can establish this unity and decide whether it has been achieved. What must be stressed here above all is that the subject has an absolute right to be judged in this matter on the basis of its *intention,* meaning an absolute right to be judged solely according to a law that it has recognized as legitimate, that it has *thought* itself: "The right of the subjective will is [to demand] that whatever it is to recognize as valid shall be seen by it as good" (*PhR* §132, 126; Knox, 86).[36] If this is the case, we can clearly see why Hegel for once speaks admiringly of Kant: "Only with Kantian philosophy has consciousness of the will won a foundation and starting point owing to the thought of its infinite autonomy" (*PhR* §135, 130; Knox, 89–90).[37] He acknowledges Rousseau's merit for similar reasons in the course of a discussion on the principle of the individual will, although he does not hold Rousseau in high regard elsewhere: "Rousseau had the merit of establishing as the principle of the State a principle that has *thought* not only as its form (e.g., the social instinct, or divine authority) but also as its content, namely, Thinking itself [*Das Denken*], that is, will" (*PhR* §258, 243 ff.; Knox, 156–57).[38] There is no denying that Hegel will criticize Rousseau later on for having transformed the State into a contract, as well as for concentrating all his attention on the individual will as if the other aspect of the will—rational objectivity—did not exist. Or that his praise for Kant is followed by a remark to the effect that adopting the perspective of Kantian abstract morality only leads to the pure verbiage of "duty for duty's sake," with

36. "Das *Recht* des *subjectiven Willens* ist, daß das, was er als gültig anerkennen soll, von ihm *als gut eingesehen* werde."

37. "[W]ie denn die Erkenntnis des Willens erst durch die *Kantische* Philosophie ihren festen Grund und Ausgangpunkt durch den Gedanken seiner unendlichen Autonomie gewonnen hat."

38. "[H]at *Rousseau* das verdienst gehabt, ein Prinzip, das nicht nur seiner Form nach (wie etwa der Sozialitätstrieb, die göttliche Autorität) sondern dem Inhalte nach Gedanke ist, und zwar das *Denken* selbst, nämlich den *Willen* als Prinzip des Staats aufgestellt zu haben." Notice the phrase "*Thinking itself,* that is, *will.*"

the consequence that no concrete deontology can possibly be established. Nevertheless, his reservations do not detract from the fact that "[moral] conscience is the expression of the absolute justification of subjective self-consciousness, namely, [its right] to know in itself and by itself what is just and what is its duty and to give recognition only to what it knows in this way to the Good, [which it expresses] at the same time by the claim that what it knows and wants in this way is just and good in *truth*" (*PhR* §137, 132–33; Knox, 91).[39]

What this means is that one can rightly demand from a man only what reason recognizes as fitting for a free *and* rational being, or, to put it more accurately, rationally free and freely rational. But it is no less the case that moral consciousness [*la conscience morale*],[40] precisely because it represents the inviolable sanctuary of interiority, is essentially ambiguous; it can be sincere just as easily as it can be deceitful, just as the *subject* can be good or bad. Because moral will is nothing but a *particular will,* it takes but a simple appeal to the agent's personal conviction for anything to be justified by subjective moral consciousness, any means to be defended as deserving the title noble or good, and any hypocrisy or any untruth to be championed.

In other words, there is no concrete morality outside a concrete situation. The will must be brought to understand that there really *is* something called the Good, that freedom *exists* in the world *objectively,* and that action *has* a meaning. The empty will and formal Good must be brought to recognize themselves as actually realized, realized

39. "Das *Gewissen* drückt die absolute Berechtigung des subjektiven Selbstbewußtseins aus, nämlich *in sich* und *aus sich* selbst zu wissen, was Recht und Pflicht ist, und nichts anzuerkennen, als was es so als Gute weiß, zugleich in der Behauptung, daß, was es so weiß und will, in *Wahrheit* Recht und Pflicht ist."

40. [The French word *conscience* has two possible translations in both English and German: "consciousness" / "Bewußtsein" and "conscience" / "Gewissen." In the above passage from Hegel, Weil has to add the adjective *moral* to *conscience* in order to specify that the word he is translating is *Gewissen* and not *Bewußtsein*. However—and although the word *conscience* serves as an equally valid translation—I have preferred to translate his noun phrase "la conscience morale" as "moral consciousness" so that its connection with all the other forms of consciousness with which Hegel is concerned is clear. TRANS.]

more or less perfectly, to be sure, but above all realized in the world, in what Hegel calls *Sittlichkeit* (concrete ethics): the moral life as lived in history, custom, the ensemble of rules, values, attitudes, and characteristic responses that together make up what we call tradition and civilization.

However, if individual consciousness can only come to recognize itself in this concrete world, it must indeed be the *individual* consciousness that recognizes itself. There is no concrete ethics or tradition that can force men to do so or that can suppress the rights of rational and formal morality. Concrete ethics is the realization of freedom; it is the vital ambiance in which a man is recognized as possessing moral consciousness by others and thereby discovers the content of this consciousness that permits his own to act, assume concrete responsibilities, and realize the Good. This concrete ethics, furthermore, makes it possible for him to realize the Good because *this Good already exists,* because there is a preexistent human world of real freedom that gives our lives their fundamental orientation. The individual does not make his entrance into a morally vacuous world. He does not find himself before the shapeless matter of duty, to which his actions then give form. Just as he did not create property as such but at most his own property and did not create morality as such but at most his own morality because they were already in existence before him, he comes to understand himself through the freedom of his will, but this understanding is completely dependent on the fact that in the world in which he lives and which lives in his reason comprehension and freedom were already in existence before him. His reflection must begin with the most denuded and abstract of materials in order to advance to an understanding of the concrete, which is the indispensable foundation for the very existence of the abstract and abstraction themselves. He must make himself negativity, and in his consciousness—both moral consciousness and self-consciousness, which are nothing but the same unique self-consciousness—he must come to have total confidence that negativity possesses absolute power and is justified by eternal right. But the meaning of this negativity is not to reach out for isolated contents that can be destroyed and consumed as soon as they present themselves; its meaning is to be found in the understanding that whatever is in the moral world, in the world of men, is the work of negativity itself and that positive law—not any and every individual positive law—is the victory of negativity over the immediate, over nature, which is present both within men and in the world outside them, and that they can abandon themselves freely and completely to the positivity of life insofar as, and only insofar as, it is the result of negativity, insofar as it is rational reality.

*Chapter Three*

# The State as the Reality of the Moral Idea

It is often claimed that right and morality are unimportant topics for Hegel; after all, does he not label them abstract? Are they not realized and given a concrete meaning only in the State? It bears repeating that this objection is based on a misunderstanding of Hegel's terminology. In Hegelian terms, that a notion is abstract does not in any way mean that it is false or that it can or must be abandoned. On the contrary, it indicates that it is indispensable—though incomplete—in every respect. It is an essential element figuring in the comprehensive account of the development of the concept, and this account will have to, as Hegel says, *aufheben* the abstract quality, which means to abrogate it, but only in the sense of abrogating what is abstract in it in order to preserve it by sublimation and thereby give it its positive function in the organized totality of Reason.

As for the problem of morality, once we set aside our prejudices and look at how science and theory actually operate in the real world, it is hard to see why his position has been so difficult to accept. There would seem to be a general consensus, now as in the past, that the rights of the individual can only be realized in a supra-individual organization and that moral life is only possible according to what we call today a "value system," which predates the individual and within which a certain range of perspectives are available, but not a perspective on the system as a whole (unless he decides to adopt the only viable form of skepticism, which abstains from any action whatsoever and retreats into total silence). Whenever man has thought of himself in larger terms, as a property-owning being, or interpreted himself as a moral consciousness, the reaction has always been that what was being interpreted and doing the interpreting was already man as he is completely and that this self-interpretation was therefore a pure abstraction. It has always been assumed—although from time to time there have been those who were pleased to affirm the contrary—that there is no such thing as MAN, only men, each with their different sexes, ages, social positions, occupations, belonging not to THE COMMUNITY but to a community, family, village, association, or country. When Hegel says that man is free, he means that in a free State he can own, use, consume, and live peacefully with other men, from which it follows that he will not recognize as valid for himself anything that is not the result of his own rational decision. This freedom is consequently that of a rational man who will only accept a universal decision to be properly his own when it seeks the universal Good, a rational decision that is the decision of man in the individual. But freedom cannot be real except in a rational world, in a world already (i.e., historically) organized in the family, in society, in the State.

❧ ❧ ❧

In our analysis of these concrete forms of moral life we shall not continue to follow, as we have until now, Hegel's outline of their development. This outline is familiar to everyone: in the family man is no longer abstract; as a member of a living unity the individual, secure in the feeling of being loved, leads a concrete existence that is also a free existence because it is an existence to which he has consented. But the family, which is still partially rooted in nature, in the immediate givens of biological individuality and the aleatory force of personal affection, does not last, and with the death of the parents the adult child is transformed into a *private person* who pursues his own ends. This individual *labors* [*travaille*], and through his labor he *socializes* himself, labor being the social mediation of man and nature. Hence property is assimilated into the family's wealth, and this in turn must merge with social wealth, in which the person participates by means of his personal wealth. In this way society is organized by, for, and in labor—divided into the estate (*Stand*) of those who labor in immediate contact with nature (agriculture), the estate of those who live by the labor of transforming and distributing (industry, trade), and the estate of those who organize the labor of the rest of society and who are free of labor in the first and second senses either because of their personal fortune or thanks to funds disbursed to them by society. Each of the estates is separate, but if the society in which he lives is free the individual, any individual, can become a member of any of the estates if his abilities permit.

It is also society (Hegel sometimes calls it the free and rational State—we shall see why later—to contrast it with the State based on necessity and understanding [*Not- und Verstandsstaat*]) that creates the first consciously developed form of organization, with the judiciary system deciding disputes between private persons, the governmental machinery of law and order [*la police*] protecting the interests of all individuals, and the corporations organizing the different forms of labor.[1] We shall not deal at any length with this part of Hegel's discussion because, on the one hand, we are eager to begin our examination of his theory of the State and, on the other hand, the topic of society as it figures in Hegel's conception of the State will be taken up further on. Thus there will be no need to respond to the traditional objection that even if the manner in which the *Philosophy of Right* describes society meets with our approval, it is rendered meaningless because its theory of the State finally comes to supersede everything that preceded it. I have already stated my reasons for dismissing this objection. But I prefer to move on to safer ground, so instead of challenging a well-ensconced tradition, let us now turn to the Hegelian State.

Here is what Hegel says about the State:

> The state is the reality of the ethical idea [*sittliche Idee*], the
> moral spirit qua revealed will manifest to itself, substantial,

---

1. [Hegel's word *Korporation*, retained by Weil, refers to professional, class, and interest groups, something akin to a medieval guild, and not a large business organization. TRANS.]

thinking and knowing itself, accomplishing what it knows and insofar as it knows it. It exists immediately in its customs and tradition [*Sitte*] and mediately in the self-consciousness of the individual, in the latter's knowledge and activity, and by virtue of his conviction [*Gesinnung*] the individual enjoys his substantial freedom in it [the State], which is his essence, end, and product of his activity. (*PhR* §257, 241; Knox, 155) [2]

The state is rational in and for itself inasmuch as it is the reality of the substantial will, a reality it possesses in a particular self-consciousness raised to the level of universality. This substantial unity is an absolute unmoved end in itself [*Selbstzweck*], [an end] in which freedom attains its most exalted right, just as this final end [*Endzweck*] attains its most exalted right with respect to individuals, whose supreme duty is to be a member of the state. (*PhR* §258, 241–42; Knox, 155–56) [3]

All the essential points can be found in these two paragraphs. The moral idea as it exists in the shape of the family and in society is only revealed as *thought* [*la pensée*] in the State. The private person acts, but although his action does not aim at the universal, it realizes the universal nevertheless. A member of society labors, and by laboring for himself he labors for everyone, but he does not understand that his labor is universal and that the world of labor is therefore a world *external* to its inhabitants, a world that is made but does not will itself to be made. Reason is present in the State because the citizen is a "particular self-consciousness raised to the level of universality," and

2. "Der Staat ist die Wirklichkeit der sittlichen Idee—der sittliche Geist als der *offenbare,* sich selbst deutliche, substanzielle Wille, der sich denkt und weiß und das, was er weiß und insofern er es weiß, vollführt. An der *Sitte* hat er seine unmittelbare, und an dem *Selbstbewußtsein* des Einzelnen, dem Wissen und Tätigkeit desselben seine vermittlte Existenz, sowie dieses durch die Gesinnung in ihm, als seinem Wesen, Zweck und Produkte seiner Tätigkeit, seine *substantielle Freiheit* hat."

3. "Der Staat ist als die Wirklichkeit des substanziellen *Willens,* die er in dem zu seiner Allgemeinheit erhabenen besonderen *Selbstbewußtsein* hat, das an und für sich *Vernünftige.* Diese substantielle Einheit ist absoluter unbewegter Selbstzweck, in welchem die Freiheit zu ihrem höchsten Recht kommt, sowie dieser Endzweck das höchste Recht gegen die Einzelnen hat, deren *höchste Pflicht* es ist, Mitglieder des Staats zu sein."

the State is the will of man insofar as he wills rationally, insofar as he wills (to recall the Hegelian definition) free will. The Hegelian State can do without any mythic or magical hypostasis to accomplish this because its reality is to be found in the consciousness of individuals, of *persons,* who by virtue of this very consciousness cease to be purely private persons. The State enjoys a real existence in the patriotic feeling of its citizens in the same way that the citizen becomes concretely free by recognizing in the State his concrete freedom, that is—it amounts to the same thing—the field of rational action. But only the State has ends that are both conscious and universal. More important still, in its essence it has more than a variety of ends; it has one sole end, the end beyond which no other end is conceivable: reason and the realization of reason, freedom.

But although the meaning of these Hegelian assertions is clear, it also seems, or at least it has often seemed, to have dangerous implications. The State is reason realized; it is positive freedom outside of which no concrete freedom is conceivable. Since the forces arrayed against the State are therefore reduced to opinion, individual desire, and the platitudes of the understanding, what is left of what one ordinarily understands by the term *freedom?* Very little, one might say. The individual will no longer counts for anything, at least if one believes that the individual will is as self-sufficient as it supposes itself to be. Moral consciousness is *aufgehoben,* sublimated, realized, preserved, what you will, but it has also lost its role as the ultimate arbiter of moral action.

*  *  *

Perhaps nothing can better illustrate Hegel's attitude in this area than his theory of how State and religion are related. Religion claims that the Truth is to be found in religion, that every human action falls under its jurisdiction, that faith, feeling, and consciousness are forbidden to submit to any earthly judge. The analogy between religious and moral problems is striking.

It is clear that we cannot enter here into a discussion of Hegel's position on religious questions.[4] Deciding whether he was a believing Christian or an atheist is primarily a biographical question. Thus, it is easily resolved and there is no reason to doubt the sincerity of his declarations, which are repeated in all of his works, in each new preface to the editions of the *Encyclopedia,* in his reviews, and in his letters to friends and to the ministry [of religious affairs]. That sincerity would not prevent us from judging that his version of Christianity was not the true one or arguing that his system is objectively atheistic — provided that we gave a suitable definition of atheism. Whatever turn the discussion takes, it is nonetheless true that Hegel always considered himself to be a Christian and that he always took the trouble to demonstrate that none of his theses were contrary to faith.

How does he elucidate the relations between the State based on thought [*L'Etat de pensée*] and the religion of freedom (which is how he sees Christianity)? The answer is to be found in two principles. The first declares that Christianity is the religion of truth and freedom. The second rejects any theory of "double truth."[5] Consequently, if both thought and religion alike have freedom and the infinite value of the individual as their essential content, no contradiction between the two can possibly arise.[6] But precisely because Christianity is the religion of truth and freedom, not only can it potentially but it must necessarily become thought [*il doit se penser*].[7] As religion, it is realized [*il se réalise*] in the form of a *representation,* of an image, but it is also a representation that continually admits and demands translation

4. Hegelians on the Left and the Right still debate this issue as hotly as ever. See Kojève, *Introduction to the Reading of Hegel,* for the "atheistic" interpretation. For the "Christian" interpretation see H. Niel, *De la médiation dans la philosophie de Hegel* (Paris, 1945); Kojève's review of Niel's book (in *Critique* 1 [1946]: 339 ff.), which gives a full presentation of the "atheistic" point of view; and Niel's review of Kojève's book (ibid. 3 [1947]: 426 ff.).

5. [In medieval philosophy the notion of "double truth" refers to the recognition that the truths of faith and reason might both be true and still be in contradiction, with those of faith finally taking precedence. TRANS.]

6. See the long discussion of the problem in *PhR* §270, to which should be added the important note to §552 from the *Encyclopedia,* 3d ed.

7. [Literally, "it must think itself." The French reflexive has a double meaning, both active as well as passive, that cannot be reproduced in English. TRANS.]

into the language of the concept. And since Christianity is composed of freedom and truth, a State without Christian foundations will not be a State based on freedom [*Etat de la liberté*].

But it is for that very reason that religion has nothing to do with the State. "The divine spirit must penetrate the worldly spirit immanently";[8] religion must not be something separate, transcendent, or superior in relation to the State because then the State would not be a Christian State.[9] The faith of the individual is inviolable, but only as long as it remains an inner faith. Action belongs to the world: "It is not enough that religion commands us 'Give unto Caesar what is Caesar's and to God what is God's,' because the question is precisely to know what belongs to Caesar."[10] If, then, there is a conflict between the representatives of religion and the State—a conflict that can only be over superficial issues given that they have identical foundations— it is the State that must have the final word because it is the State that represents thought and reason over against images and feeling and is the (rational) reality of (representational) faith.

Furthermore, Hegel rejected any Church intervention in political affairs with a vehemence that did him nothing but harm in the "most Christian" Prussia of Frederick-William IV and the two Williams.

> Religion is a relation to the Absolute that takes the form of feeling, representation, faith; and at its heart, which embraces everything, everything only exists as an accident that could just as well not exist . . . From those who "are looking for God" and are assured that they know everything *immediately* in their un-

8. "Der göttliche Geist muß das Weltliche immanent durchdringen" (*Encyclopedia*, 2d ed., 468).

9. Closely analogous to this conception of the Christian State—since as a Christian State it has no need to defer to a separate religious authority—is Hegel's view that the State based on Right and laws [*l'Etat du droit et de la loi*] does not institute the judiciary as a separate constitutional branch of government, precisely because law is this State's very soul.

10. "Es ist nicht genug, daß in der Religion geboten ist: *Gebt dem Kaiser, was des Kaisers ist, und Gott, was Gottes ist;* denn es handelt sich eben darum zu bestimmen, was des Kaisers sei, d.i. was dem weltlichen Regimente gehöre" (*Encyclopedia*, 2d ed., 468). [Weil does not translate the final clause, "what belongs to worldly rule." TRANS.]

schooled opinions, instead of undertaking the labor of raising
their subjectivity to consciousness of the Truth and to knowledge of duty and objective right, [from those] can only result
the destruction of all ethical relations, stupidity and abomina-
tion . . . [It is true that] the State cannot concern itself with
content inasmuch as it is part of the inwardness of representation . . . [and that] the proper domain of doctrine is in the
conscience and consists of the right of self-consciousness to
subjective freedom—this sphere of interiority which as such is
not the domain of the State . . . [But] mind as free and rational
is ethical [*sittlich*] in itself . . . the veritable idea is *real* [*wirklich*]
reason, which exists as the State . . . In contrast to the *faith* and
authority [of the Church] in matters of concrete ethics, right,
laws, institutions, in contrast to the Church's *subjective conviction,*
the State is that which knows [*das Wissende*] . . . the principle of
its form qua universal is essentially thought. (*PhR* §270, 258–72;
Knox, 166–72)[11]

The State has the authority to judge the actions of the Church
and Churches because it thinks and because it *knows*. It is the State,
and the State alone, that acts in full consciousness, it alone that organizes freedom in the world. It *is* this organization; it does not *make*
it, which would mean that the State was something other than the

---

11. "Die Religion ist das verhältnis zum Absoluten *in Form des Gefühls, der Vorstellung, des Glaubens,* und in ihrem alles enthaltenden Zentrum ist alles nur als ein
Accidentelles, auch Verschwindendes . . . Von denen, die den *Herrn suchen* und in
ihrer ungebildeten Meinung alles *unmittelbar* zu haben sich versichern, statt sich die
Arbeit aufzulegen, ihre Subjektivität zur Erkenntnis der Wahrheit und zum Wissen
des objektiven Rechts und der Pflicht zu erheben, kann nur Zertrümmerung aller
sittlichen Verhältnisse, Albernheit und Abscheulichkeit ausgehen . . . Auf den In-
halt, insofern er sich auf das Innere der Vorstellung bezieht, kann sich der Staat nicht
einlassen . . . Die *Lehre* selbst aber hat ihr Gebiet in dem Gewissen, steht in dem
Rechte der subjektiven Freiheit des Selbstbewußtseins,—der Sphäre der Innerlichkeit, die als solche nicht das Gebiet des Staates ausmacht . . . Die Entwicklung . . .
hat erwiesen, daß der Geist, als frei und vernünftig an sich sittlich ist, und die wahr-
hafte Idee die *wirkliche* Vernünftigkeit, und diese es ist, welche als Staat existiert . . .
Gegen ihren *Glauben* und ihre Autorität über das Sittliche, Recht, Gesetze, Institutionen, gegen ihre *subjektive Überzeugung* ist der Staat vielmehr das *Wissende* . . . Weil
das Prinzip seiner Form als Allgemeines wesentlich der Gedanke ist."

organization of rational action, reason in action. It is Christian in the sense that it realizes on earth, and in a rational form, what constitutes the content of religion but in religion takes the form of a representation, experienced in the mode of feeling.[12]

12. Hegel's critique of Catholicism centers on the way its rigid separation of the sacred from the profane prevents us from understanding the State as the realization of reason:

There can be a relationship of un-freedom in the form, although the content of religion as it is in itself is absolute spirit . . . In the Catholic religion this spirit (in which God is known) is strictly opposed in reality [*Wirklichkeit*] to the self-conscious spirit. First, in the Eucharist, God is presented to religious adoration as an external thing . . . From this first relation of externality, which is the highest, flow all the other external relations, [which are] therefore without freedom, without spirit, superstitious: the estate of the laity, who receive from outside and from another estate the knowledge of divine truth and the direction of the will and moral consciousness . . . What is more, the subject gives up directly addressing God and prays to others to pray for him . . . To this principle, to this development of un-freedom in the domain of religion corresponds in the actual State a legislation and a constitution of juridical and ethical [*sittlich*] un-freedom and a state of affairs replete with injustice and immorality . . . Un-freedom of form, that is, of knowledge and subjectivity, has the consequence for moral content that self-consciousness is not represented as immanent [in moral content], that it [this content] is represented as transcending [*entrückt*] the latter in such a way that it is considered to be true only insofar as it is negative in relation to the reality of self-consciousness. In this un-truth the moral content is called the sacred. But when the divine spirit is introduced into reality, when reality is liberated [in order to go] toward it, [then] what ought to be *holiness* in the world is replaced by concrete morality [*Sittlichkeit*] . . . [according to the Catholic distinction between the profane and the sacred] the laws appear as a purely human work in this opposition over against those things declared sacred by religion . . . This is why such laws (based on rational principles), even when their content is true, fail when faced with [Catholic] moral consciousness, whose spirit is different from the spirit of the laws and does not sanction the latter . . . It is only in the [Protestant] principle of spirit, which knows its essence, which is absolutely free in it, and which has its reality in the activity of its own liberation, it is only in this principle that there exists the absolute possibility and necessity for the power of the State, religion, and the principle of philosophy to coincide, for the reconciliation of reality as such with spirit, of the State with religious moral consciousness and equally with philosophical knowledge, to be accomplished . . . Thus the concrete morality [*Sittlichkeit*] of the State and the religious spirit of the State offer solid and mutual guarantees for each other.

(*Encyclopedia,* 3d ed., §552, esp. 466 and 469. See also *Philosophie der Weltgeschichte,* vol. 4, *Die Germanische Welt,* 889, 899 ff.; and *PhR* §270, 257 ff. [Knox, 164 ff.]).

According to Hegel, no compromise is possible between Catholic transcendence

What Hegel says about religious *feeling* is also valid for moral reflection. The earthly supremacy of the State derives from its spiritual content: it realizes its political sovereignty because it realizes spirit and freedom, "the infinite value of the individual." As I have already pointed out, Hegel acknowledges that there can be tyrannical States, unjust States, or States that are retrograde in relation to the spirit of their age, and we shall see later how these States are summoned before the tribunal of history and condemned. But here, where our main concern is with the criticisms of his "statism" and "moral relativism," we must first consider what Hegel says about a legitimist and absolutist theory both founded and founding the concept of the State on the concept of power. The *Philosophy of Right* devotes a long note to the theorist of the Restoration, Carl Ludwig von Haller, who would later become the favorite theorist of Frederick-William IV, that romantic on the throne of Prussia. Here is the paragraph that expresses with perfect clarity what reason means in the context of the State:

> Reason . . . consists as far as its content is concerned in the unity of objective freedom, that is, of substantial and universal will, and subjective freedom qua the knowledge of the individual and the will that pursues its particular ends; and this is why, as far as its form is concerned, it [reason] consists in an activity [*Handeln*] that determines itself according to laws and principles that are thought and so universal. (*PhR* §258, 242; Knox, 156) [13]

---

and the modern State, which is only a modern and a rational State inasmuch as it realizes in living reality what religion opposes to earthly existence as transcendent principle. For Hegel there is no Catholic State that is also rationally free because Catholic consciousness considers the State to be essentially immoral (or amoral). Freedom can be imposed on a Catholic people, but if it is imposed, the people will not be able to recognize it as moral (i.e., as a realization of freedom). However inaccurate Hegel's description of Catholicism may be, it does provide evidence that he is far from conceiving the State as purely a power apparatus. For him, the *defective* State is characterized by an imposed authority and the lack of a morality centered on freedom.

13. "Die Vernünftigkeit besteht . . . konkret dem Inhalte nach in der Einheit der objektiven Freiheit . . . des allgemeinen Gesetzen und Grundsätzen sich bestimmenden Handelns."

Freedom is law to the extent that the law is rational, that it expresses the content of the individual rational will, and that it presents itself as a principle that is *thought* [*principe pensé*] and is thinkable and that therefore both can be and is given recognition and consented to [*reconnu*] as such by the citizens.

What does Haller say? That the divine order—more modern "thinkers" of the same school will speak of the order of nature or of life—desires the supremacy of the strong over the weak, the great over the small; that the law and laws only serve to distort this relationship that God has commanded; that, from another point of view, everything is therefore for the best since the feeling of one's own superiority elevates the character of the great and produces in the master precisely those virtues most advantageous for his inferiors. Is this really the Word of God? asks Hegel.

> But the word of God very definitely distinguishes its revelations from the apophthegms of nature and natural man . . . Herr von Haller should have bewailed as the hardest of God's punishments that of being led astray from [the way] of thought and reason, of respect for the laws, and of the knowledge [that teaches] that it is of infinite importance and that it is divine [to know] that the duties of the State and the rights of the citizens, as well as the rights of the State and the duties of the citizens, are determined *by the law*—to have been led so astray that he took absurdities for the word of God . . . The hatred of law, of right established by the law, is the *Shibboleth*[14] whereby fanaticism, idiocy, and the hypocrisy of good intentions are clearly and infallibly revealed and recognized for what they are. (*PhR* §258, 249n; Knox, 158–60)[15]

14. See Judges 12:5–6.
15. "Das Wort Gottes unterscheidet vielmehr seine Offenbarungen von den Aussprüchen der Natur und des natürlichen Menschen sehr ausdrücklich . . . Hr. v. H. hätte es aus Religiosität vielmehr als das härteste Strafgericht Gottes beweinen müssen,—denn es ist das Härteste, was dem Menschen widerfahren kann,—vom Denken und der Vernünftigkeit, von der Verehrung der Gesetze und von der Erkenntnis, wie unendlich wichtig, göttlich es ist, daß die Pflichten des Staates und

The essence of the State is law, not the law of the strongest, the law of the royal pleasure, the law of "natural generosity," but the law of reason, in which every rational being can recognize his own rational will. It is true that the State appears to the spheres of private right, of the family, even of the social world of labor as an eternal necessity, as a superior force. But "on the other hand, it is their *immanent* end, and its strength lies in the unity of its own ultimate end with the particular interest of individuals, in the fact that individuals have duties to the State insofar as they also have rights . . . Slaves have no duties because they have no rights, and vice versa" (*PhR* §261, 252; Knox, 161–62).[16]

What troubles contemporary sensibilities (note that I say *sensibilities,* not analytic faculties) is the link made between freedom and reason, the thesis that there is no political freedom outside of reason, that individual preferences and *convictions,* with their individuality, nonuniversality, and pretension to exercise a freedom against reason, cannot be publicly recognized [*reconnues*] by the State. But the fact is that in one and the same breath *personal conviction* claims both to constitute the moral law and yet to be liable to error. Nothing else matters except that I have recognized such and such a maxim or principle as my own, and yet if I do not want to fall into absolute skepticism or nihilism, I will claim at the same time that my conviction could well be mistaken. However, the State cannot be satisfied with convictions, good or bad, since it is the entire reality of organized life:

> Conscience is subject to the judgment whether it is true [*wahrhaft*], and its appeal to its ipseity [*sein Selbst*] is in immediate opposition to what it wishes to be, namely, the rule of ratio-

die Rechte der Bürger, wie die rechte des Staats und die Pflichten der Bürger *gesetzlich* bestimmt sind, soweit abgekommen zu sein, daß sich ihm das Absurde für das *Wort Gottes* unterschreibt . . . Der Haß des *Gesetzes, gesetzlich* bestimmten *Rechts* ist das Schiboleth, an dem sich der Fanatismus, der Schwachsinn und die Heuchelei der guten Absichten offenbaren und unfehlbar zu erkennen geben." [The final sentence of the above-quoted passage precedes the others in Hegel's text. TRANS.]

16. "Andererseits ist er ihr *immanenter* Zweck und hat seine Stärke in der Einheit seines allgemeinen Endzwecks und des besonderen Interesses der Individuen, darin, daß sie insofern *Pflichten* gegen ihn haben, als sie zugleich Rechte haben . . . Sklaven haben deswegen keine Pflichten, weil sie keine Rechte haben; und umgekehrt."

nal action, valid in and for itself, and universal. For this reason, the State cannot give recognition to conscience in its specific form, that is, as subjective knowledge, any more than science can grant validity to opinion, [simple] affirmation, or the appeal to a subjective opinion. (*PhR* §137, 133; Knox, 91) [17]

[Because] whoever wills to act in this reality [of the world] has *eo ipso* submitted himself to its laws and recognized the right of objectivity. (*PhR* §132, 127; Knox, 88) [18]

Neither the State nor, for that matter, any other organization can rely on moral conscience, purely individual judgments, or personal conviction. This is not because their doing so would disappoint our liking for philosophically rigorous structures but because otherwise there would be no State at all. Freedom can only be expressed by the State; it is the State that is or is not the realization of freedom. The individual's freedom remains purely arbitrary insofar as he refuses to recognize the universal and the objectivity of the law and tries to maintain himself in an individuality that has not gone beyond the subjective.

The State embodies reason to counter this arbitrariness. To counter the feeling, *representation,* and image of faith, it ensures that the rational content of religion is fully developed in the service of reason. It furnishes the only content that could give man the possibility of living morally in order to fill the void of purely *moral* reflection and provides a still vital and historical tradition with the self-consciousness that it was lacking. This is because the State is reason in and by the law. Not by a transcendent and mysterious law but

17. "Das Gewissen ist daher diesem Urteil unterworfen, ob es *wahrhaft* ist oder nicht, und seine Berufung nur *auf sein Selbst* ist unmittelbar dem entgegen, was es sein will, die Regel einer vernünftigen, an und für sich gültigen allgemeinen Handlungsweise. Der Staat kann deswegen das Gewissen in seiner eigentümlichen Form, d.i. als *subjektives Wissen* nicht anerkennen, so wenig als in der Wissenschaft die subjektive *Meinung,* die *Versicherung* und *Berufung* auf eine subjektive Meinung, eine Gültigkeit hat."

18. "Wer in dieser Wirklichkeit handeln will, hat sich *eben damit* ihren Gesetzen unterworfen, und das Recht der Objektivität anerkannt."

by its operative laws, by its universal administration of private and particular affairs, by the thought it devotes to the increasingly pure elaboration of the principles of a free existence, of a form of community that satisfies every thinking citizen, every educated and civilized (*gebildet*) man[19] who has left behind the gross materiality of immediate desire as well as the passivity of pure sacrifice so as to be able to raise himself to the rational thought *(verständig)* that perceives all interests as interdependent. The State can be called free if the rational citizen can find in it the satisfaction of his desires and rational interests, interests that he can justify to himself insofar as he is a thinking being; if the citizen recognizes in the laws of the State the expression of feelings and tradition that have guided him (even when he was not aware of it); if the laws are not only just from the point of view of an enlightened despot but can and must be recognized as such by all those who desire justice, by those who seek their liberation from all immediate givens, including their own empirical, natural, and given character, by those who have understood that the natural man is not free, that only the rational and universal being can be free. The State is rational because it speaks universally, for each and every one of its members, in its laws, and because everyone finds whatever constitutes the meaning, value, and honor of his existence recognized in its laws.

We are certainly free to refuse reason, just as we are free to assert anything we please. But if we do so, we thereby deprive ourselves of the means to convince and refute others and to speak rationally of the State. We can choose passion over will, arbitrary decision [*l'arbitraire*] over freedom. But then we must be consistent (for the sake of the discussion) and agree that for our part we are opposed to the State, any State, that we would abolish all and any principles of organization and any positive freedom, any freedom to act, plan, or realize and find satisfaction in rational action, which is the rational organization of the community and of all communities of men.[20]

19. See *PhR* §187.

20. This gives us the opportunity to refer again to Malinowski's *Freedom and Civilization,* where one finds an excellent critique of the negative conception of freedom and a fine discussion of "positive" freedom, both based on a scientific reflection that becomes philosophical unconsciously and despite itself.

## Chapter Four

# The Constitution

The previous chapters have established that the Hegelian State is grounded in freedom and always acts with the interests of freedom in mind. To quote one of Hegel's contemporary disciples, the *Philosophy of Right* "is completely made out of the pure steel of freedom."[1] I have already made the case that the traditional portrait of Hegel as a political thinker does not square with the reality. Now do we not have the right to take the next step and say that this portrait, curiously, bears virtually no resemblance to the sitter? It cannot even be compared to one of those caricatures in which we catch a glimpse of the original beneath its deformed features because they capture, though in a more striking and less natural form, those of the real person's face. And if this portrait is so defective, are we not then obliged to seek the reasons for this intriguing fact, if only to know to what degree Hegel himself is responsible for the mistake?

One reason that is easily adduced: Hegel felt that the Prussia of 1815–20 was a realization (more or less imperfect—the question remains open) of the State based on freedom. There are many commentators who will say that the Prussia of Frederick-William IV, that of William I and Bismarck (in other words the Prussian State as it developed after Hegel's death), was anything but a State based on freedom [*un Etat de la liberté*], in which case Hegel must have been a devotee of the authoritarian State and it must have been to further its cause

---

1. E. Gans, quoted in Haym, *Hegel und seine Zeit*, 369.

that he gave it the spurious title "rational State" [*Etat de la raison*]. The flaws in this reasoning, which arise from its anachronism, are only too transparent and predictable.

But all the same, are they not a little too glaring to be completely wrong? Is there nothing in the specific ordinances of Prussian constitutional law that might justify the attacks first made in 1840, at the latest in 1848, and continuing up to our own time? Might they be justified by the contradictions between the principle and its applications? What indeed *is* the concrete reality of the Hegelian State?

It is this: a monarchy, more precisely a constitutional monarchy, provided with a strongly centralized administration,[2] whose economic activities are for the most part decentralized, with a body of professional civil servants, no State religion, and absolutely sovereign internally as well as externally. It is the modern State as it exists today everywhere in the world, with one difference: the present insignificance of the monarchic principle (admittedly anything but insignificant in Hegel's eyes). We shall have occasion to discuss this later, but first let us try to give a detailed view of what Hegel understood by the term *constitution*.

European legal theorists in the nineteenth century, influenced by the ideas produced by the French and American Revolutions, conditioned us to think of the constitution as a juridical act, a document drawn up after due deliberations, discussions, and votes by either the people or their representatives, or both. This is completely alien to Hegel:

> Since spirit is real only as what it knows itself to be, and the State, as the spirit of a people, is both the law permeating all its [internal] relationships and also the tradition [*Sitte*] and consciousness of the individuals it comprises, the constitution of any given nation depends in principle [*überhaupt*] on the mode of being [*Weise*] and the degree of the intellectual and moral culture [*Bildung*] of this people's self-consciousness. It is in its self-consciousness that its subjective freedom and thus the

2. [For the specific meaning of *administration* in Weil see ch. 1, n. 15. TRANS.]

reality [*Wirklichkeit*] of its constitution resides. The proposal
to give a constitution—even one more or less rational in content—to a nation a priori would be an idea [*Einfall*] overlooking
precisely that moment in a constitution that makes it more than
a purely mental object [*Gedankending*]. Hence every nation has
the constitution that is suitable for it and that it deserves. (*PhR*
§274, 281; Knox, 178–79)[3]

It is difficult to resist the temptation to write constitutions and thus
prescribe by statute the one and only way of ensuring the nation's
well-being. But since freedom can only be realized to the degree that
it is to be found in the self-consciousness of the people, since, more
simply put, any group of men asks for what it desires and not what
it ought to desire, and since the State can only be organized on the
basis of concrete patriotism—the real feeling of its citizens, feeling
that has genuine content—its only possible realization may be one in
which reason and freedom figure to a lesser degree, that is, one that
will appear of lesser value to those who judge it from the point of
view of a more completely realized freedom.

Who is to frame the constitution? This question seems clear, but
closer inspection shows it to be absurd for it presupposes that
there is no constitution, but only a mass of atomic individuals
brought together. How could a mass of individuals acquire a
constitution, whether on its own or with outside help, by benevolence, by thought, by force? A solution would have to be
left to the mass itself since the concept has nothing to do with a
mass. But if the question presupposes an already existent consti-

3. "Da der Geist nur als das wirklich ist, als was er sich weiß, und der Staat, als
Geist eines Volkes, zugleich das *alle seine Verhältnisse* durchdringende Gesetz, die Sitte
und das Bewußtsein seiner Individuen ist, so hängt die Verfassung eines bestimmten
Volkes überhaupt von der Weise und Bildung des Selbstbewußtseins desselben ab;
in diesem liegt seine subjective Freiheit, und damit die Wirklichkeit der Verfassung.
Einem Volke eine, wenn auch ihrem Inhalte nach mehr oder weniger vernünftige
Verfassung a priori geben zu wollen,—dieser Einfall übersähe gerade das Moment,
durch welches sie mehr als ein Gedankending wäre. Jedes Volk hat deswegen die
Verfassung, die ihm angemessen ist und für dasselbe gehört."

tution, then *framing* really means nothing but modifying. (*PhR* §273, 280–81; Knox, 178)[4]

Thus, constitutional history cannot be said to have a beginning; there is no prior set of conditions preceding the social contract. Men have always lived in organized, previously constituted societies, and the constitution is a reality that precedes any theory. Wherever a constitutional document exists (Great Britain has managed without such a document to this day) it can be drawn up more or less well, more or less clearly, but it will only be effective if it corresponds to the real and historical constitution, to the constitution of the nation. So the first step in understanding must be to take the word *constitution* in its *physiological* sense.[5]

But although it may be a historical and living reality, indeed because of this very fact, the constitution is not an object that cannot be penetrated by scientific understanding. For it is an organization of freedom, a rational organization, and the fact that the constitution of a given State remains, inevitably, at an earlier stage of development than that reached by the thought of an epoch does not in any way render such understanding impossible. All that is necessary and sufficient to achieve it is an accurate knowledge of the constitution of a free State [*un Etat libre*] at this particular moment of history. Admittedly, this summit of political development has not been reached everywhere, but lower levels of development will only ever be understood by first analyzing the higher ones. One must begin there.

The State is the reality [*Wirklichkeit*] of concrete freedom, but concrete freedom entails that the individual person [*persönliche*

4. "Wer die Verfassung machen soll? Diese Frage scheint deutlich, zeigt sich aber bei näherer Betrachtung sogleich sinnlos. Denn sie setzt voraus, daß keine Verfassung vorhanden, somit ein bloßer atomistischer *Haufen* von Individuen beisammen sei. Wie ein Haufen, ob durch sich oder andere, durch Güte, Gedanken oder Gewalt, zu einer Verfassung kommen würde, müßte ihm über lassen bleiben, denn mit einem Haufen hat es der Begriff nicht zu tun.—Setzt aber jene Frage schon eine vorhandene Verfassung voraus, so bedeutet das *Machen* nur eine Veränderung."

5. The idea is taken from Montesquieu, to whom Hegel makes specific reference (see *PhR* §3, 7; Knox, 16).

*Einzelheit*] and his particular interests achieve their complete development and recognition of its right-for-itself—as they do in the sphere of the family and civil society—and also, on the one hand, that they [individuals and their interests] pass over [*übergehen*] of their own accord into the interest of the universal and, on the other hand, that they recognize the universal by means of their knowledge and will and [recognize it] as their own substantial spirit and that they act with the universal in mind as their final end in such a way that the universal neither has any value nor achieves completion without the interests, knowledge, and will of particulars and individuals do not live for the latter [particular interest] as [simple] private persons . . . The principle of modern States possesses this prodigious strength, this depth, that it allows the principle of subjectivity to progress to its culmination in the extreme, the autonomous extreme, of personal particularity and yet at the same time brings it [the principle of subjectivity] back to the substantial unity and so maintains this substantial unity in itself. (*PhR* §260, 251; Knox, 160–61)[6]

The modern State, therefore, has the peculiar characteristic that its citizens are not its subjects, *subditi,* that reason and organization do not present themselves to them as a foreign and incomprehensible will, but that it is they themselves who, without abandoning their individuality or their concrete interests, recognize in the objective universal the accomplishment of this individuality and these interests

6. "Der Staat ist die Wirklichkeit der konkreten Freiheit; die *konkreten Freiheit* aber besteht darin, daß die persönliche Einzelnheit und deren besondere Interessen sowohl ihre vollständige *Entwicklung* und die *Anerkennung ihres Rechts* für sich (im Systeme der Familie und der bürgerlichen Gesellschaft) haben, als sie durch sich selbst in das Interesse des Allgemeinen teils übergehen, teils mit Wissen und Willen dasselbe und zwar als ihren eigenen *substantiellen Geist* anerkennen und für dasselbe als ihren *Endzweck tätig* sind, so daß weder das Allgemeine ohne das besondere Interesse, Wissen und Wollen gelte und vollbracht werde, noch daß die Individuen bloß für das letztere als Privatpersonen leben . . . Das prinzip der modernen Staaten hat diese ungeheure Stärke und Tiefe, das Prinzip der Subjektivität sich zum *selbständigen Extreme* der persönlichen Besonderheit vollenden zu lassen und zugleich es in die *substantielle Einheit zurückzuführen* und so in ihm selbst diese zu erhalten."

of theirs, just as, conversely, the reality of the State is not dependent on the will of a single master (or masters). In other words, the modern State is essentially different from the Roman Empire, in which the citizen was recognized by the State in his capacity as a free individual ("private person") but where the individual had no role in the State, which was itself real and present only in the person of the emperor (not to mention the existence of slaves, human beings who are not considered men in the eyes of the law). The modern State does not confine its citizens in its organization; it is *their* organization.

*  *  *

If it were my aim to provide an analysis of Hegelian thought that did justice to its profound unity, now would be the time to discuss the fundamental concept of *satisfaction*. Satisfaction is the ultimate cause of human history. It assigns history its end: the point at which each individual is *recognized* as an absolute value by every other individual and by all individuals, when, to recall another Hegelian concept, *mediation* between men — and between men and nature — will be total.[7] Here I shall have to limit myself to this simple allusion to the Hegelian system, which will be sufficient to help us understand in what sense the modern State gives satisfaction to its citizens: each individual knows himself to be recognized, each individual is and *knows himself to be* an active member of the community and knows in addition that he is known and recognized as such by all the other members and by the State itself.

This principle allows Hegel to show how the concrete organization of the State can be developed from the concept of freedom. Since individuals' particular interests are realized in the State and duties are imposed on them only insofar as they possess rights, it becomes pos-

7. For more on the concepts of recognition (*Anerkennung*) and satisfaction (*Befriedigung*) see Kojève's analysis in *Introduction to the Reading of Hegel*, which relies on passages taken from the *Phenomenology of Spirit*.

sible to describe how the State, defined as a rationally organized unit, manages to organize itself rationally.

What is necessary for this to happen? First, a branch of government that determines the universal universally: the legislative branch. Then the branch of government that subsumes the particular case under the universal rule, applies the laws and principles, and decides cases in everyday reality: the administration. Finally, the authority that formulates the empirical will, that, after due deliberation and discussion, after conflicting interests and doctrines have been given a hearing, declares its fiat: the branch of government that makes decisions, the sovereign, the prince.

It is this final element of the Hegelian constitution that has caused the most damage to his reputation over the last century and in the first half of our own. How can anyone be a monarchist? Certainly, Hegel's position can be perfectly well explained by the history of the period. The epoch in which Hegelian thought developed witnessed the defeat of the republican principle: the two great revolutions in England and France both ended with the restoration of the monarchy, and around 1820 one would not have found a single republic of any significance in Europe. (Switzerland and the Hanseatic towns only owed their independence to the rivalries of the great powers.) But the Hegelian thesis deserves to be judged according to the criteria of reason, which it claims to be its own. And it comes as a surprise that viewed from that angle it is convincing. After all, what is the prince? The individual who decides. How does he decide? Certainly not as a particular will, according to a course of action determined by a particular interest, and even less as an arbitrary will. If he were to do so, he would not be a prince but a tyrant: "Despotism generally means the absence of laws, in which the particular will as such, whether it is that of a monarch or a mob (ochlocracy), has the force of law or replaces law with force" (*PhR* §278, 284; Knox, 180).[8]

The prince, like all the other branches of the State, represents the

8. "Der Despotismus bezeichnet überhaupt den Zustand der Gesetzlosigkeit, wo der besondere Wille als solcher, es sei nun eines Monarchen oder eines Volks (Ochlokratie), als Gesetz oder vielmehr statt des Gesetzes gilt."

universal; and equally like them, he represents a distinct moment, an essential function, but one that must not be understood as independent of the other branches, even less as essentially opposed to, mistrustful of, and in competition with them for influence. He expresses the sovereignty that becomes concrete in him, and thereby present in the world, and it can only become so according to the law of this world: it can only become real in the shape of a human individual.

Hegel deduces the superiority of hereditary monarchy from this. And it is perhaps the only significant concession to the official opinion of his time that he ever made because, strictly speaking, the deduction only proves the necessity that *some* unspecified concrete individuality be the incarnation of the will that decides. Hegel has reflected on how difficult it is to shield the "head of State" from all particular interests, which would inevitably be able to exert a powerful influence over him if he had come to supreme power by means of an election. This was how he argued against elections in a note accompanying the ontological argument.[9] But chiefly, and in my opinion this is the veritable reason, the essential function of the Hegelian prince is to represent the almost biological continuity of the State.[10]

Whatever Hegel's views were on the principle of hereditary monarchy, what his critics have conveniently forgotten is that there can be no State without an individual representative of sovereignty. It might be claimed that this representative does not have a very important role to play, that the presidents in most republics and the monarch in Great Britain and the other European monarchies of our own time only occupy the position of head of State in a formal sense. But what indeed is the role of the Hegelian prince in practice? Certainly he is sovereign: it is he who decides in the last instance, who pardons criminals, who is commander in chief, who declares war, signs laws, and settles disputes between his ministers, all of whom are chosen by him personally. But we would have to wilfully disregard everything Hegel says about the State to believe that these very extensive powers

9. See *PhR* §281, esp. the explication.

10. Or at least this is the most plausible conclusion to draw from the emphasis Hegel puts on *Natürlichkeit* (of natural becoming and being) in *PhR* §280.

could ever be exercised without the consent and against the interests of the nation. Furthermore, they could only be exercised with a view to what the nation understood to be its interest. It is not the prince who determines the problems, it is not the prince who elaborates possible solutions, it is not even the prince who effectively decides which of the possible solutions to implement, since to reach this decision too he is obliged to act only after consulting his ministers.

To show that this interpretation is not merely a well-contrived but specious rebuttal, here is what Hegel says about the issue in one of his lectures on the *Philosophy of Right* (in which he made statements for which the romantic royalists never forgave him):

> In a perfectly organized State, it [the king's role] is only a matter of a final point of formal decision and a natural bulwark against passion. It is wrong therefore to demand objective qualities of a monarch. He only has to say yes and dot the i's. For this final point of decision making should be constituted in such a way that it is not the particularity of the character that counts. (*PhR* add. to §280; Knox, 288–89) [11]

We can glean from this addition that possibly Hegel tended to be more radical in his lectures than in his publications; but what it proves beyond a doubt, precisely to the degree that it is not really adding anything substantial to the texts that were actually published, is that the prince is neither the center nor the principal mechanism of the State. The power of decision rests with the king, but it is not he who decides when or what will be decided; he can say no, but it is not up to him to invent, create, or govern. Whose role is it then?

We have now reached a far more troublesome area for those who want to defend Hegel against the liberals' charges. If there is one point on

---

11. "So ist eben die Voraussetzung hier nichtig, daß es auf die Besonderheit des Charakters ankomme. Es ist bei einer vollendeten Organisation des Staats nur um die Spitz formellen Entscheidens zu tun und um eine natürliche Festigkeit gegen die Leidenschaft. Man fordert daher mit Unrecht objektive Eigenschaften an dem Monarchen; er hat nur Ja zu sagen, und den Punkt auf das I zu setzen. Denn die Spitze soll so sein, daß die Besonderheit des Charakters nicht das Bedeutende ist."

which Hegel stated his opinions without the slightest ambiguity, it is his opposition to popular sovereignty. The expression itself is not meaningless, he says, but as a way of understanding the organization of the State and the nature of political action it is useless, indeed dangerous.

> We may speak of popular sovereignty in the sense that a people constitutes an autonomous entity and a State of its own vis-à-vis the outside world . . . We may also say of domestic sovereignty that it resides in the people, if we are speaking of the whole in general in the sense we demonstrated above, that sovereignty rightfully belongs to the State. But popular sovereignty understood as something opposed to the sovereignty existing in the prince . . . is one of those confused ideas based on the wild imagination [*wüste Vorstellung*] of the people. Taken without its monarch and the organization of the whole, which necessarily and immediately goes with it, the people are a formless mass, no longer a State and no longer possessing any of those determinations that are to be found solely in the whole when it is internally organized: sovereignty, government, courts, hierarchy, representative estates. (*PhR* §279, 288; Knox, 182–83) [12]

What does this mean? At first glance it would seem to assert unambiguously that the people (in the familiar sense the word has acquired

12. "*Volkssouveränetät* kann in dem Sinn gesagt werden, daß ein Volk überhaupt *nach außen* ein Selbständiges sei und einen eigenen Staat ausmache . . . Man kann so auch von der *Souveränetät* nach *innen* sagen, daß sie im *Volke* residiere, wenn man nur überhaupt vom *Ganzen* spricht, ganz so wie vorhin gezeigt ist, daß dem *Staate Souveränetät* zukomme. Aber Volkssouveränetät als im *Gegensatze gegen die im Monarchen existierende Souveränetät* . . . gehört . . . zu den verworrenen Gedanken, denen die *wüste* Vorstellung des *Volkes* zugrunde liegt. Das Volk, ohne seine Monarchen und die eben damit notwendig und unmittelbar zusammenhängende *Gegliederung* des Ganzen genommen, ist die formlose Masse, die kein Staat mehr ist und der *keine* der Bestimmungen, die nur in dem *in sich geformten* Ganzen vorhanden sind,—Souveränetät, Regierung, Gerichte, Obrigkeit, Stände und was es sei,—mehr zukommt."

On this point (as on all the others) the National Socialists took the opposite view to that expressed in Hegel's doctrine.

in contemporary political parlance) have no role to play in the constitution of the State or in political action. A brief glance at what I said earlier about the free constitution should be enough to show that nothing is further from the truth: only a constitution according to which each citizen possesses rights proportional to his duties and knows that by laboring for the whole he is laboring for himself can be considered modern. Moreover, Hegel's analysis of how the State is organized (which we will come to in due course) makes this abundantly clear. So why is Hegel's critique still expressed with such violence? No doubt it was fueled by his suspicion of revolutionary movements. But if we take a closer look at the revolution against which Hegel was voicing his opposition, it turns out, surprisingly, to have been the revolution of *nationalism,* the revolution of Greater German nationalism, to be exact, the very same that unleashed the movement of 1848, that won its first partial victory with Bismarck and went on to win a second, total this time but short-lived, with Hitler. Even if it were not impossible to read Hegel's texts in any other way,[13] the exasperated remarks of modern critics of Hegel would plainly confirm this interpretation. From the first of these critics, Haym, up to the most recent, Rosenzweig, who accused the Hegelian idea of being "hard and narrow" and in 1914 had voiced his hope that the "suffocating narrowness of Bismarck's Reich" would make way for a "Reich breathing the free air of the whole world," they all readily acknowledge that Hegel was an implacable opponent of the Greater German idea—which is no surprise since the liberals in nineteenth-century Germany, the fathers of the Second Reich, were themselves first and foremost nationalists.[14] As they see things—and there is no difference between them and the National Socialists on this score—the people give themselves a State. For Hegel, it is the State and history—which

13. I am not speaking here of "social revolution," which we shall look at later on.
14. In the *Philosophie der Weltgeschichte,* vol. 4, *Die Germanische Welt,* 906 ff., Hegel says that "Germany, whose ultimate destiny is spiritual, has not been able to achieve political unity . . . In its relations with the external world Germany is a nullity." His use of "spiritual" indicates that Hegel, like Goethe, sees in its political weakness Germany's true power.

become indistinguishable once a people has emerged from barba-
rism—that form [ *forment* ] [15] the people.[16]

However, if I am right and Hegel's criticism of popular sovereignty
has ethnic nationalism as its principal target, if, on the contrary,
Hegel was prepared to recognize the people's sovereignty insofar as
it is organized, forms a State, and feels this State to be the highest
expression of its own life, then this other type of sovereignty must
be expressed somehow in the construction of the political system.
The prince expresses and incorporates sovereignty, so what is left for
the people? Parliament, or to use the Hegelian term, the *estates*. The
people deliberate, and deliberate according to the constitutive divi-
sions making up society, that is, through their respective *estates*: the
estate of labor in direct contact with nature, represented by the great
landowners, which takes the shape of an Upper Chamber, made up
of men who sit in it by virtue of their birth or their landed holdings;
and the estate of non-landowning members of society, represented by
delegates acting on their own responsibility, without a fixed mandate,
but reposing on the trust and confidence of their constituents—deputies, certainly, but not necessarily elected, since they do not represent
individuals but objective interests, corporations, or parishes.

So the people do have a say in government. But at first we cannot help feeling that in this State everything is arranged in such a
way that the people's voice will not be able to make itself heard. And
the whole system becomes all the more suspect when we turn our
attention to the role played by the administration, the civil service,
in this constitution. For the principal authority that we were look-

15. [The French *former* means "to educate" as well as "to create." The English *to
form* still retains some of the French's plastic force, so I have retained it at the risk
of being accused of Gallicism. TRANS.]

16. It is curious to note that Hegel's thesis turned out to be perfectly right; in
particular it accurately predicted the course of German unification, which came
about in the teeth of the national-liberal ideals of 1848 and at the hands of a servant
of the Prussian Crown, Bismarck. It was he who created the new *national-liberalism*
of Empire.

ing for so desperately, which is not held by the crown nor governed by popular representation, is right here in the hands of the civil servant. It is he who prepares everything, determines what the problems are, and works out all the solutions. Responsible to the head of State alone, properly qualified by his education (with standards ensured by State examinations), by his knowledge, by his experience of affairs, the civil servant is the veritable servant of the State—and its veritable master. Essentially objective, essentially apolitical (where *political* would mean taking a partisan position), recruited without any regard for background, wealth, or social status, the civil servant, unlike the farmers and members of the other professions, does not belong to either of the *political estates.* How could he possibly sit in Parliament, since the chambers' primary function is to oversee the activities of the administration? But he *is* part of a *social estate,* the universal estate (*allgemeiner Stand*), the most influential of all the estates. While it is nothing politically, the civil service is everything with regard to the organization of the State; it constitutes the second branch of government, the active branch of government, situated between the sovereign and the legislature. It is true that the prince decides; it is also true that the chambers vote on laws and decide on issues of universal import. But of the three branches it is ultimately the administration that enjoys a preponderance of power in relation to the other two. It cannot be put in stronger terms than those used by Hegel himself:

> The way ordinary consciousness imagines it at first . . . is generally something like this: the representatives of the people, or even the people themselves, must know best what is in their best interest and have the best will for attending to their own Good . . . Now, the people, if this term is taken to mean a particular group of the citizens of a State, constitutes that group which does not know what it wills. To know what one wills, and still more to know what the will that exists in and for itself, that is, reason, wills, this is the fruit of profound knowledge and insight, which are precisely the things that are *not* characteristic of the people. When we reflect on the matter, we find that the

guarantee of the common good and public freedom represented by the estates does not reside in their particular insight [*Einsicht*], because the highest civil servants necessarily have a deeper and more comprehensive insight into the nature of the State's institutions and requirements and, moreover, a greater skill in and habituation to the business of government, so that they *can* achieve what is best without the estates, as they also continually have to do while the estates are in session. This guarantee depends in part, it is true, on the *supplementary* understanding of the deputies, an understanding above all of the activity of officials who operate at some distance from the eyes of the higher functionaries of state and in particular of the more pressing and particular needs and deficiencies they experience in a concrete fashion; but, from another point of view, it resides in the effect produced by anticipation of censure from the great numbers of the people, a censure that is, moreover, public, [which means] that the greatest understanding must be used in the public presentation of government affairs and plans and that everything must be carried out exclusively in accordance with the purest motives . . . But with regard to the particularly good will of the estates aimed at the common good . . . it is the view of the people and in general the negative point of view that assumes beforehand the government's bad or less than good will, an assumption that . . . would call for the countercharge that the estates, which are made up of isolated individuals, of private points of view and particular interests, are inclined to devote their activities to these interests at the expense of the general interest. (*PhR* §301, 309–10; Knox, 196)[17]

17. "Die Vorstellung, die das gewöhnliche Bewußtsein . . . zunächst vor sich zu haben pflegt, ist vornehmlich etwa, daß die Abgeordneten aus dem Volk oder gar das Volk es am *besten verstehen* müße, was zu seinem Besten diene und daß es den ungezweifelt besten Willen für dieses Beste habe . . . So ist das vielmehr der Fall, daß das *Volk,* insofern mit diesem Worte ein besonderer Teil ausdrückt, *der nicht weiß was er will.* Zu wissen, was man will, und noch mehr was der an und für sich seiende Wille, die Vernunft, will, ist die Frucht tiefer Erkenntnis und Einsicht, welche eben

This quotation is long, but it offers us the possibility of summarizing in one place the full significance of Parliament and its role in the Hegelian State: no direct elections; representation of society's interests by delegates that today we would think of as belonging to "corporations"; parliamentary functions limited to two, namely, supervision of the administration (although Hegel thinks this oversight is more effectively exercised by the administration's own internal hierarchy) and, through their power to pass or veto legislation, citizens' participation in the State in the sense that they are cognizant of the fact that the affairs that remain for all practical purposes in the hands of the administration are *their* affairs and are being conducted in their best interest and with their consent; in the form of Parliament they are recognized by the State and in the State for what they are concretely, that is, according to their participation in the labor of the society. The individual is never given an order to which he has not consented; but what is asked of him is this consent, not his initiative.

In whatever way an individual finds in the fulfillment of his duty equally his personal interest, satisfaction, reward, and posi-

---

nicht die Sache des Volks ist. —Die Gewährleistung, die für das allgemeine Beste und die öffentliche Freiheit in den Ständen liegt, findet sich bei einigem Nachdenken nicht in der besonderen Einsicht derselben—denn die höchsten Staatsbeamten haben notwendig tiefere und umfassendere Einsicht in die Natur der Einrichtung und Bedürfnisse des Staats, sowie die größere Geschicklichkeit und Gewohnheit dieser Geschäfte und *können* ohne Stände das Beste tun, wie sie auch fortwährend bei den ständischen Versammlungen das Beste tun müssen, —sondern sie liegt teils wohl in einer Zutat von Einsicht der Abgeordneten, vornehmlich in das Treiben der den Augen der höheren Stellen ferner stehenden Beamten, und insbesondere in dringendere und speziellere Bedürfnisse und Mängel, die sie in konkreter Anschauung vor sich haben, teils aber in derjenigen Wirkung, welche die zu erwartende Zensur Vieler und zwar eine öffentliche Zensur mit sich führt, schon im voraus die beste Einsicht auf die Geschäfte und vorzulegenden Entwürfe zu verwenden und sie nur den reinsten Motiven gemäß einzurichten ... Was aber den vorzüglich guten Willen der Stände für das allgemeine Beste betrifft ... so ... gehört es zu der Ansicht des Pöbels, dem Standpunkt des Negativen überhaupt, bei der Regierung einen bösen oder weniger guten Willen vorauszusetzen; —eine Voraussetzung, die ... die Rekrimination zur Folge hätte, daß die Stände, da sie von der Einzelnheit, dem Privatstandpunkt und den besonderen Interessen herkommen, für diese auf Kosten des allgemeinen Interesses ihre Wirksamkeit zu gebrauchen geneigt seien."

tion in the State, a right must arise for him whereby the *res publica* becomes his own particular affair. I am not suggesting that particular interests should be neglected or, even less, that they should be completely suppressed; but they should be made to harmonize with the universal, for it is in this way that they can be preserved as well as the universal. The individual, who is a subject insofar as his duties are concerned, finds in the fulfillment of his duties as a citizen [*Bürger*] the protection of his person and property, due regard for his private welfare, and the satisfaction of his substantial being, the consciousness and feeling of himself as a member of the whole; and, [on the other hand] it is in fulfilling these duties by, performing tasks and undertaking services for the *State,* that he finds his preservation and perdurance [*Bestehen*]. (*PhR* §261, 253–54; Knox, 162)[18]

Parliament must satisfy this demand. Through Parliament the citizen can make his complaints heard, express his needs, participate in universal decisions, that is, legislation, exercise a supervisory function with respect to the application of these decisions by the local administration, convince himself that the affairs of the State are his and that his affairs are those of the State to the degree that his labor and his interest contribute to the common interest. Parliament can truly be said to unite the State as administration [*l'Etat-administration*] with the sphere of social labor [*la société du travail*].

But the State remains the State, society remains society. The citizen

18. "Das Individuum muß in seiner Pflichterfüllung auf irgendeine Weise zugleich sein eigenes Interesse, seine Befriedigung oder Rechnung finden, und ihm aus seinem Verhältnis im Staat ein Recht erwachsen, wodurch die allgemeine Sache *seine eigene besondere* Sache wird. Das besondere Interesse soll wahrhaft nicht beiseite gesetzt oder gar unterdrückt, sondern mit dem Allgemeinen in Übereinstimmung gesetzt werden, wodurch es selbst und das Allgemeine erhalten wird. Das Individuum, nach seinen Pflichten Untertan, findet als Bürger in ihrer Erfüllung den Schutz seiner Person und Eigentums, die Berücksichtigung seines besonderen Wohls und die Befriedigung seines substantiellen Wesens, das Bewußtsein und das Selbstgefühl, Mitglied dieses Ganzen zu sein und in dieser Vollbringung der Pflichten als Leistungen und Geschäfte für den Staat hat dieser seine Erhaltung und sein Bestehen."

labors and organizes his own labor; the civil servant administers the whole of society in its unity. In order for the latter to administrate effectively, it is necessary, on the one hand, that the former see in the administration the defender of his interests and on the other, that the administration be well informed about the nature of these interests. It is therefore essential that the administration defend the common interest in a competent fashion, furnished with a full knowledge of the facts and the professional training required to enable the citizenry to go about their labors in tranquillity. If society is therefore the basis, the matter—which in this instance does not mean a substance lacking form—of the State, self-conscious reason will only be found in the State itself. Outside it can exist concrete morality, tradition, labor, abstract right, feeling, and virtue, but not reason. The State alone thinks, the State alone can become thought completely.[19]

So nothing is more false in Hegel's eyes than the theory that states that the State should defend society. Certainly, there is no State without society. For Hegel this is as true as it is banal. But it is only in the State that society is organized according to reason. Society itself recognizes this—does not the State sometimes require of its citizens that they sacrifice their property and lives when it is engulfed in a struggle for its very existence, which is equally the concrete existence of the citizens' and society's rational freedom?

> When this sacrifice was called for, the calculations would come out wrong if the State were regarded as nothing more than civil society and its final end [defined as] protecting the security of life and property; for this protection cannot possibly be realized by the sacrifice of what is supposed to be protected—on the contrary. (*PhR* §324, 332; Knox, 209)[20]

19. ["Seul l'Etat pense, seul l'Etat peut être pensé totalement." The final clause is in the passive voice and can be literally translated "only the State can be thought totally," a sentence that is unhelpfully ambiguous in English. TRANS.]

20. "Es gibt eine sehr schiefe Berechnung, wenn bei der Forderung dieser Aufopferung der Staat nur als bürgerliche Gesellschaft, und als sein Endzweck nur die Sicherung des Lebens und Eigentums der Individuen betrachtet wird; denn diese Sicherheit wird nicht durch die Aufopferung dessen erreicht, was *gesichert* werden soll;—im Gegenteil."

* * *

The State—Hegel seems to care about nothing else. And this is a State based on administration [*l'Etat de l'administration*], the State of civil servants. In the event, is not the violent opposition of the liberals to Hegel's theory of much greater significance than that of the partisans of Prussian and German unification? Hegel's principles may have emerged unscathed from the liberals' critique, but is the same true for the consequences of the principles? This question must be given a precise meaning, since we are doing philosophy and must satisfy the canons of objective thought. The issue here is not whether Hegel's State is "attractive" or "unattractive"; the important thing is whether once the principles had been granted, the right conclusions were made. In this case, we are hard put to find the logical mistake that proves that the Hegelian theory is worthless due to some basic error. And the theory's consequences, now that we have accepted them, are not favorable for liberal thought.

Let us take a single example: the case of public opinion. Hegel does not deny its existence or importance. But in his eyes *public* opinion is the realm of *particular* and irresponsible opinions, and the less true they are the more irresponsible and particular they must be considered. If public opinion is on the one hand *vox Dei* in that it expresses "the true needs and authentic tendencies of reality" (*PhR* §317, 323; Knox, 204), on the other it is the veritable kingdom of error. For opinion to be able to make informed decisions, it would by definition need to possess the knowledge it lacks, even if it always acted with the best of intentions. No doubt, as Hegel puts it, it is easy to highlight the sinister side of any legislation meant to control the press, and he adds that it is even impossible for it not to make us wary. What is more, precisely because the offensive acts committed by opinion are subjective in character, they resist being described in objective terms, and any condemnation will itself take on from the target its character of subjective judgment. It would also be correct to say that propaganda addresses itself to men's freedom and that without their acquiescence its discourse would never be translated into real action. All of this is irrelevant to Hegel. The interest "of individuals, society, and the State" (*PhR* § 319, 328; Knox, 207) has the right to be defended against the arbitrariness of irresponsible expression, just as it has the right to be defended against any religious or bogusly scientific doctrines that endanger it.[21]

Hegel's position is shocking, and it would be easy to succumb to the temptation of calling him an advocate of the autocratic or police State. But in his defense we can not only refer to the constitutional guarantees of freedom provided in the Hegelian State, to the rule of law, to the recognition of the absolute value of the individual, to parliamentary oversight; it is simpler and more persuasive to take a look at the political reality of modern States that are called free.

What is obvious from the outset is that there is no longer a single State of any importance whose essential heart is not to be found in its administration. Even the Anglo-Saxon empires, which managed to avoid it for so long, have ended up by creating large bodies of civil servants destined to defend what Hegel calls the common interest, that is, the interest not of society, not of a group of individuals, not even of all the individuals making up society, but of the State as a historical and sovereign entity. There are no longer any States that are truly parliamentary in the nineteenth-century sense of the word. Even in those cases where the constitution has retained this form, the reality is far closer to Hegel's description, what with the role of the unions, of industrial, agricultural, medical associations, and so on, with economic councils, autonomous organizations in which the *estates* of society meet and marshal their actions in common, with the representation of corporate interests by their delegates who hale from corporations and are given legitimacy by their corporations' confidence in them. The citizen counts on these organizations and their

21. Science has no more right than the Church to set itself up outside of the State and consider the latter a simple means to obtain its own ends (*PhR* §270, 267; Knox, 170); but it is not placed under censorship because it is not one of the factors in political life that act by insinuation, etc., on public opinion and because generally it is of a different nature than opinion (*PhR* §319, 327; Knox, 207). However, their position does not protect the members of university departments if they undermine the foundations of the State with spurious teachings (*PhR* xvi; Knox, 8).

spokespersons to be "reconciled with the State," far more than on their individually elected representatives. Thus latter-day parliaments are nothing more than the expression of the unity or conflict of concrete interests and are perfectly incapable of exercising authority when confronted by a coalition of the principal corporate interests. If necessary, they are only too happy to put themselves in the hands of governments, which have taken the place of the prince, and the bureaucracy, which has a full grasp of the situation, problems, and means of action. There is only a difference of degree between "democratic" States and the "authoritarian" States in this area, their essential difference being determined by the role of objective and rational law, that is, by the possibility given or denied to the citizens to take part in the supervising, formulating, and developing of social and economic policy, by the possibility of determining their own lives. But there is no modern State in which individual and State live in an unmediated relationship with one another, the desideratum of the theory that goes back to Rousseau; the relationship is always socially mediated.

So Hegel was right, and in this sense history itself has come to his defense. Even in his views on public opinion he was only describing what is still the case for us today. Every State passes laws to protect the personal honor of its citizens, good morals, the form of the constitution, the head of State, and public credit. If we have become especially sensitive to any encroachments on the freedom of the press, it is because we are dealing with a problem that Hegel could not have even dreamed of: a press totally controlled by the government or at the disposal of private interests powerful enough to influence and bias public opinion. Hegel did not foresee such a possibility because for him public opinion was tantamount to the expression of opinion emanating from society—a society in which monopoly was as yet unknown. It was radically separate from the government and enjoyed only one sort of relationship with it: mutual supervision.

To sum up: the Hegelian theory of the State is correct because it provides a correct analysis of the State as it was in Hegel's time and in ours.

## Chapter Five

# The Character of the Modern State

We can now conclude. Hegel is not Prussia's philosopher, unless he deserves that title because he was opposed to the rising tide of Greater German nationalism. He is the philosopher of the modern State, and his analysis of it is the correct one. It indicates precisely what constitutes freedom in the State and what conditions it must fulfil to be considered a State based on freedom, one that realizes modern thought. It only remains for us to make our excuses for not having given a more complete analysis of the *Philosophy of Right* in political terms. (As for my failure to provide an analysis of Hegel's ontology and an examination of the ultimate foundations of his political theory, I have already made my apologies above.)

For instance, should we not have discussed the third social *estate,* in which courage is paramount? Would our argument not have been strengthened by insisting that while Hegel gives the professional army an important place in the State and recognizes in the soldier the autonomy of a being who is purely *for himself* [*pour soi*] in the face of death, ascribing to him the supreme decision in the immediate presence of spirit, he at the same time sees in this greatness a state of stupidity, an existence dominated by a purely external automatism, and the absence of any of the spirit inherent in the individual?[1] And would this not lend further confirmation to our interpretation, namely, that Hegelian philosophy has virtually no resemblance to what is understood nowadays by the word *Prussian?*

1. See *PhR* §§325 ff., esp. §328.

But there is a more significant problem, perhaps the most disturbing of all: if Hegel's analysis is correct, does this not leave it vulnerable to the most serious and decisive criticism? If Hegel has described, and if he wanted to describe, the State in itself, the idea of the State, does it not then follow that for Hegel history has reached its appointed end by producing a State that satisfies reason, meaning free will, that nothing more needs to be done in this world, and that the future can only be an empty and tedious continuation of the present?

\* \* \*

The interest recently shown in the *Phenomenology of Spirit* certainly has not always served to advance our understanding of Hegelian thought, although this interest has been extremely valuable in itself because it has encouraged all lovers of philosophy to take a closer look at this truly great philosopher. It is too easily forgotten that Hegel finished the *Phenomenology* at the time of the battle of Jena. The "world soul" that Hegel saw passing under his window was not yet the Napoleon of Tilsit, the Napoleon of Spain or Moscow; above all it was not the Napoleon of St. Helena. We all know what Napoleon's fate was to be in the decade following Jena. It is impossible that the man for whom reading the newspapers was "the morning prayer of the modern gentleman" would have been indifferent to these subsequent developments. Napoleon fell; the highest point of history was not attained; the world empire of Spirit that crowned the development portrayed in the *Phenomenology of Spirit* was not realized. Is it credible that Hegel then simply replaced Napoleon with Frederick-William III, and the Empire with Prussia? Would the total reconciliation of man with himself as the culmination of a fully completed series of mediations simply be replaced by a conception depicting a system of nation States, sovereign, independent, in conflict with one another, continually returning or on the verge of returning to their brutal struggle, the same violence that mediation was supposed to eliminate?

And yet this is exactly what recent commentators have been saying: Hegel was a conformist in Berlin and then he was a *collaborator* in Jena and Bavaria. It would be useless to remind them of all the evidence to the contrary that has been presented so far, or to add that Hegel's State is not as absolute as has been claimed, that the morality of the individual in it has an absolute value within the limits of its own domain, that the sphere of social labor has its rights upon which the State should not infringe, that the latter is nothing but a realization of the historical nation, that the individual is not in any way sacrificed to a totalitarian Moloch, that for Hegel religion, art, and science are forms of spiritual existence superior and not inferior to the State,[2] that the State cannot transgress its limits without losing its legitimacy, which consists precisely in its rational character. Doubters will remain unconvinced until we demonstrate that Hegel's theory does more than erect simple safeguards and voice reservations, until, more precisely, we demonstrate that Hegel considered the State outlined by the *Philosophy of Right* to be itself a *historical* phenomenon, not only in the sense that each State exists in history but in the sense that the very form of the State is only transitory, a form beyond which, at this point in time, spirit has not yet progressed, but which is neither unsurpassable nor definitive. Only in this way will the problem posed by Hegel's politics finally be resolved.

❋ ❋ ❋

The *Philosophy of Right* concludes with a few paragraphs giving a rapid sketch of the Hegelian philosophy of history. They contain nothing of great interest, and the presentation is identical to those of the *Encyclopedia* and the *Introduction to the Philosophy of History*[3]—nothing of interest, that is, except that this particular sketch is to be found in this particular place. Hegel makes the transition to it in the most natural way, by introducing the concept of State sovereignty in the areas of foreign policy and war. The State, says Hegel, is not defined by its domestic sovereignty alone; it is not entirely made up of legisla-

2. See the final paragraph of the *PhR;* a more explicit demonstration can be seen in the very structure of the *Encyclopedia.*

3. Which has come to us in the form of a manuscript in Hegel's hand (see the editor's remarks in the Lasson edition).

tive and executive sovereignty. It is, and is *essentially,* an individuality among others, an irreducible and complete individuality. And since among individuals there can only be immediate relations until some superior unity is instituted above them, no concrete laws can be applied to States governing the relationships they have with each other. At most there is an extremely simple and tenuous moral tie between modern States: mutual recognition. And since this recognition is of fundamental importance to both parties, even the violent conflict that is always a possibility wherever relations between individuals are immediate and natural cannot be allowed to cancel out this essential recognition and make them forget that the normal relation between individuals who have given each other mutual recognition is peace, in other words that the possibility of peace must always be preserved. "War includes the norm of the *jus gentium,* [which requires] that in war the possibility of peace be preserved, that, for example, envoys therefore be respected, and that in general war not be waged against domestic institutions, against peaceful family and private life, or against private persons" (*PhR* §338, 341–42; Knox, 215).[4]

States have a further moral obligation, according to Hegel: the treaties that sovereign States have signed and by which they are thereby mutually obligated should be strictly observed.[5] What is striking in these two rules is the appearance of the word *duty.* States are bound to each other by a moral concept, by duty. Could it be any more obvious that we have returned in this instance to the abstract and inferior form of morality that preceded the concrete morality of a universally recognized tradition, a fortiori a form inferior to the State rationally organized by means of the universal and conscious sovereignty of its laws? In the same way that the moral individual can choose between good and evil, the State, which *is free* to act in

4. "Er [der Krieg] enthält damit die völkerrechtliche Bestimmung, daß in ihm die Möglichkeit des Friedens erhalten, somit z. B. die Gesandten respektiert, und überhaupt, daß er nicht gegen die inneren Institutionen und das friedliche Familien- und Privatleben, nicht gegen die Privatpersonen geführt werde."

5. *PhR* §333. It is clear that Hegel is adopting and alluding to Kant's theses (see Kant, *Project for Perpetual Peace,* in *Immanuel Kant: Perpetual Peace and Other Essays,* ed. and trans. Ted Humphrey [Indianapolis, 1983], 107–43).

a moral fashion, *is free* also therefore to act in an immoral fashion. It *must* observe its treaties, but whether it *does* in fact do so depends on its particular and empirical will alone. "Since the sovereignty of a State is the principle of relations between States, they therefore find themselves in a state of nature in relation to each other, and their rights have their effective reality [*Wirklichkeit*] not in a universal will constituted so as to have power over them but in their particular wills" (*PhR* §333, 339; Knox, 213).[6]

There is a morality by which States can be judged, and it is perfectly legitimate to describe a foreign policy as immoral. But this morality is only morality and has no more power than any morality has:

> This universal provision of international law [i.e., *pacta esse servanda*] does not go beyond stipulating a duty, the actual state of affairs will be alternatively [determined at some times by] relations that adhere to treaties and [at others] by their abolishment. There is no praetor; at most there are arbitrators and mediators between States, and even they get appointed according to the vagaries of chance, that is, depending on particular wills. (Ibid.)[7]

For the State, like any natural individual, cares only to defend its own good, and the wisdom of the State is not universal providence but only its individual wisdom. The principle of its action "is not universal, philanthropic thought but the good [of the State] when it is really injured or threatened in its determined particularity" (*PhR* §337, 341; Knox, 214–15).[8]

6. "Weil aber deren [der Staaten] Verhältnis ihre Souveränetät zum Prinzip hat, so sind sie insofern im Naturzustande gegeneinander, und ihre Rechte haben nicht in einem allgemeinen zur Macht über sie konstituierten, sondern in ihrem besonderen Willen ihre *Wirklichkeit*."

7. "Jene allgemeine Bestimmung bleibt daher beim *Sollen,* und der Zustand wird eine Abwechslung von dem den Traktaten gemäßen Verhältnisse und von der Aufhebung desselben. Es gibt keinen Prätor, höchstens Schiedsrichter und Vermittler zwischen Staaten, und auch diese nur zufälligerweise, d.i. nach besonderen Willen."

8. "Das substantielle Wohl des Staates ist sein Wohl als eines *besonderen* Staates in seinem bestimmten Interesse und Zustande und das ebenso eigentümlichen äußern Umständen nebst dem besonderen Traktaten-Verhältnisse; die Regierung ist somit eine *besondere Weisheit,* nicht die allgemeine Vorsehung . . . sowie der Zweck im Ver-

Assertions like these make it appear as though Hegel were effectively defending violence, force, and politics without fear of God or man; an enemy of morality, if not in domestic politics, at least in the State's relations with other countries. Whatever serves the interests of the individual State is called "good," and the *bellum omnium contra omnes* (the war of all against all), though banished from the domestic arena, deemed to be the normal relationship between States. The *homo homini lupus* (man a wolf to man) has been exiled from the individual State only to be reinstated in international affairs in a far more virulent form. Does Hegel himself not admit this quite openly? Does he not state that international relations take place in the context of an "extremely turbulent play of passions, interests, competing ends, natural talents and virtues, violence, wrongs and vice, as well as external chance . . . a play of forces in which the ethical *totum* itself, the independence of the State, is exposed to chance?" (*PhR* §340, 342; Knox, 215).[9]

But it is precisely this spontaneous admission that ought to give us pause. If we accept it at face value, then to the list of charges traditionally leveled against Hegel we must add cynicism or, with equal plausibility, stupidity, and nothing in Hegel's work would justify such a charge. He would not have spent his whole life defending his theory against charges of pantheism and atheism or availing himself of the slightest opportunity to insist repeatedly that in terms of content his system is identical to the purest Christian doctrine only then to proclaim suddenly that morality is nothing, and in the very domain that encompasses all the others, that of historical action. Then again, if we explained the contradiction by simple negligence on Hegel's part,

---

hältnisse zu anderen Staaten und das Prinzip für die Gerechtigkeit der Kriege und Traktate nicht ein allgemeiner (philanthropischer) Gedanke, sondern das wirklich gekränkte oder bedrohte Wohl in *seiner bestimmten Besonderheit* ist." See also *PhR* §336.

9. "In das Verhältnis der Staaten gegeneinander, weil sie darin als *besondere* sind, fällt das höchst bewegte Spiel der inneren Besonderheit der Leidenschaften, Interessen, Zwecke, der Talente und Tugenden, der Gewalt, des Unrechts und der Laster, wie der äußern Zufälligkeit . . . ein Spiel, worin das sittliche Ganze selbst, die Selbständigkeit des Staates, der Zufälligkeit ausgesetzt wird."

that would be to rely on the most unlikely of hypotheses. What are we to conclude then?

The *Encyclopedia* contains a discussion of the State that can be helpful in this matter:

> Finally, the State has as one of its aspects that of being the *immediate* reality of a *single* and *naturally* determined people. Insofar as it is an *isolated individual* it exists *exclusively* in regard to *other individuals* of the same species. Their relations give rise to the *arbitrary* and to *chance* because the universal of right *ought* to govern their relations but never *really* does so because of the autonomous totality of these *persons.*[10]

I have italicized a certain number of expressions in this quotation that contain terms to be found in texts already quoted above but not elsewhere so conveniently assembled in one place. The collection of these terms together takes on a precise meaning in the context of the Hegelian system: *immediate, single, natural, isolated individual* among other isolated individuals, *the arbitrary, chance, lack of reality, simple duty*—each of these concepts has a negative value, and their combined presence can lead us to only one conclusion, namely, that the sovereign and independent State is no more *rational* than the individual who lives under the regime of formal right and thinks in terms of abstract morality. The State is perfect; States taken individually are not. In other words, Hegel declares that there is no law between States, that morality in international relations has not yet been achieved, that its application depends on the good or bad will of the individual States. He does not say that this is a perfect state of affairs. He does not defend it; he establishes it as fact and understands it. But this understanding already contains the hopeful call—no, Hegel does not allow himself hopeful calls—a prediction, a judgment that

---

10. "Der Staat hat endlich die Seite, die unmittelbare Wirklichkeit eines *einzelnen* und *natürlich* bestimmten Volkes zu sein. Als einzelnes Individuum ist er *ausschließend* gegen *andere* eben solche Individuen. In ihrem *Verhältnisse* zueinander hat die Willkür und Zufälligkeit statt, weil das *Allgemeine* des Rechts um der autonomischen Totalität dieser Personen willen zwischen ihnen nur sein *soll,* nicht *wirklich* ist" (*Encyclopedia,* 3d ed., §545, 456).

history is moving toward total reconciliation and mediation. If this were not so, then history would be absurd, the struggle of man with nature would be endless, the labor of negativity would never succeed in assimilating the *immediate*, the *natural*, the *prior determination*, the *arbitrary, chance,* and there would be no *really existing reason* for man.

It should not be held against Hegel that he lived in a world (which has not changed much since) in which the reconciliation of man with himself, to use Hegel's words, had not been achieved. Nor should we blame him for making it his principle that history has an ultimate meaning and is no less intelligible than nature. Whether or not we agree that philosophy and science are possible, we ought to be sufficiently consistent in our own minds not to deny the possibility of science if we are simultaneously affirming that our negative claim has scientific, logical, and philosophical validity. Finally, we ought to forgive him for believing that good intentions and irresponsible opinions would change nothing in the course of the world as long as they were not *realized,* that is, not transformed into action. And we should also forgive him if he states that science deals with what is, not what ought to be—and this would be easily done if we would only be kind enough to recall that the highest reality for Hegel is that of the active, living Spirit [*l'Esprit agissant*]. Hegel justified the national and sovereign State in the same way that the physicist justifies a storm: by understanding what is rational in the phenomenon at hand. And since no one has accused physicists of being opposed to the installation of lightning conductors, it would be unfair to impute to Hegel a doctrine of political quietism. On the contrary, he thinks that the forward march of spirit has not yet come to an end, that the Berlin of 1820 is not the final destination of history, and that what he calls the idea—the negativity that is striving to realize itself as positive freedom, as the presence of satisfaction and the recognition of the infinite value of every man—has not yet revealed itself completely to the light of consciousness.

> At present the spirit of the world has come to this point . . . The succession of the forms of spirit has therefore come to a halt for

the time being . . . My aim in this history of philosophy is to offer you an exhortation, to grasp the spirit of the age, which is implanted in us by nature, and to draw it out from its natural form [*Natürlichkeit*], that is, from its closed and inanimate existence, toward the light and into the light, showing everything in its rightful place — in full consciousness.[11]

The man who chose to close his lectures on the history of philosophy with these words can hardly have believed that there was nothing left to be done in the world and that everything had reached its definitive state. No, spirit has not yet reached the clarity in which it would be completely conscious of itself; it has not yet achieved its return to itself in the freedom of real existence; the individual spirits of the peoples continue to struggle, and the day of judgment has not yet come.

* * *

This is why Hegel concludes the *Philosophy of Right* with the summary of his philosophy of history mentioned above. Spirit does not impose itself on reality by way of moral teaching, as *idealism* supposes. It informs it by its action in the world — unconscious, violent, almost a force of nature. If this were not the case, history would indeed have come to an end and reason would govern all relations in a truly universal and thus truly human organization. In history Spirit can only act through violence:

> Often it seems that it [spirit] has forgotten and lost itself, but while it is inwardly in opposition to itself, it is inwardly progressing — as Hamlet says about the spirit of his father: "Well done, old mole" [*Hamlet* 1.5.162] — to the point that once it has accumulated enough of its energies within itself, it lifts up and breaks through the earth's crust, which was separating it from the sun and its concept. When such a time has come, spirit can

11. *Vorlesungen über die Geschichte der Philosophie,* ed. H. Glockner (Stuttgart, 1928), 3:685, 690 ff.

be said to have put on its seven-league boots; the earth's crust, an edifice without a soul, worm-eaten, falls away, and spirit shows itself again in the shape of fresh youth."[12] The new form of spirit and the new organization of rational life are not created by philosophical discussion or sermons and moral lectures but by the struggle between "national spirits" and the organizing principles of freedom as they are actually present in different States. It is from the perspective of universal history that spirit judges the particular forms in which it was incorporated at one particular stage of its development [*devenir*]. "The element in which the universal spirit exists in the outside world [*Dasein*] . . . is, in world history, efficient reality [*Wirklichkeit*] in all of its interiority and exteriority." But this history "is not the abstract and nonrational necessity of a blind *fatum* but . . . the explanation and realization of the universal spirit," and States, peoples, and individuals, in their constitutions and in the whole extent of the real conditions of their existence, consciously defend their interest while all the time serving as the unconscious tools and organs of this labor going on within them, "in the course of which these forms pass away, but at the same time spirit in and for itself is toiling to prepare its passage to its next higher stage" (*PhR* §§341, 342, and 344, pp. 344–45; Knox, 216).[13]

A given people realizes quite naturally, that is, unconsciously, the form that is most perfect at a given time, the one that represents the stage presently reached in the progress of freedom. This in turn implies that this people can and must lose this supremacy as soon as

12. Ibid., 685.
13. "Das *Element* des Daseins des allgemeinen *Geistes* . . . ist in der *Weltgeschichte* die . . . Wirklichkeit in ihrem ganzen Umfange von Innerlichkeit und Äusserlichkeit" (*PhR* §341, 344). "Die Weltgeschichte ist ferner nicht das bloße Gericht seiner *Macht,* d.i. die abstrakte und vernunftlose Notwendigkeit eines blinden Schiksals, sondern weil er an und für sich *Vernunft,* und ihr Fürsichsein im Geiste Wissen ist, ist sie die aus dem *Begriffe* nur seiner Freiheit notwendige Entwicklung der *Momente* der Vernunft und damit seines Selbstbewußtseins und seiner Freiheit" (§342, 344). ". . . jenes inneren Geschäftes . . . worin diese Gestalten vergehen, der Geist an und für sich aber sich den Übergang in seine nächste höhere Stufe vorbereitet und erarbeitet" (§344, 345–46). [In this paragraph, when not quoting directly Weil is mostly paraphrasing these German passages. TRANS.]

another nation bearing a new idea appears on the scene. When this occurs, the former is just as likely to continue to exist as to perish; it can even accept the new principle, but it is no longer the bearer of spirit. It was in this manner that the Oriental, Greek, and Roman Empires succeeded one another and it is in the same manner that the Germano-Christian Empire presently reigns supreme (*PhR* §§ 347, 351 ff.).

This conception of history is familiar to us, and it is also perspicuous. But for all this, could it not be justifiably called a "mental construct," an "idealist" view of things in the worst sense of the word? It is true that spirit does not realize itself in a conscious manner. Progress is not the work of knowledge and good will; in understanding history one does not anticipate the actual events of history but is obliged to follow them. Thought never manages to go beyond spirit as it gets realized in its concrete and historical forms. Nevertheless, is this motive force of history, spirit, not a pure myth, a product of secularized theology? Possibly. It is of course true that we can only understand past history as meaningful by presupposing that it had a meaning from the beginning, and it is also true that nothing could represent a less "mystical" *meaning* for history than the realization of positive freedom, the satisfaction of man in the reality of his life. We can, indeed must, grant this; the only other alternative is nihilism. But how and in what concrete form is this quest [*recherche*] for freedom expressed, a quest whose object is history in the making [*qui se fait*], neither understood nor understandable because it is not yet over and done with [*n'est pas encore faite*]? Any final judgment about the validity of Hegel's "historical idealism" will depend on Hegel's answer to this question.

As it happens, Hegel's answer is twofold. Let us begin with the first part of his answer, in which he introduces the concept of the *hero,* since it is the part he chose to emphasize and has therefore aroused the most interest. In the *The Philosophy of History* it goes by the name *great man*.[14] It is the great men that, by pursuing their own interest,

---

14. *Die Vernunft in der Geschichte* (1837), ed. G. Lasson (Leipzig, 1931), 56 ff. (Sibree, 30 ff.). The text used here was written by Hegel himself, not taken from students'

their personal satisfaction, are at the same time "the instruments and means of something higher and more vast of which they know nothing, which they realize unconsciously."[15] Their action is not the result of dispassionate reflection on the needs of spirit, for "if we call passion an interest in which the whole individuality, with every fiber of its will throws itself into a single object to the neglect of all the other all-too-numerous interests that one could and equally does have, [an interest] on which it concentrates all its desires and energies, then we must say that generally speaking nothing great has been accomplished in the world without *passion*."[16] And these men of passion are the instruments of universal spirit because what they take to be their particular interest (and that this is really the case is shown by the fact that the crime they commit when they act against the established morality of their time [*Sitte*] has fatal consequences and destroys them in their concrete individuality) so closely matches the unconscious aspiration of all men in their dissatisfied state of existence that "the peoples rally around his [the great man's] standard; he shows them and carries out what is their own immanent tendency [*Trieb*]."[17]

The *Philosophy of Right,* more prudent in its choice of words because they were meant for publication, prefers the term *hero.* In this work the hero is not placed in direct relation to the movement of history; likewise, the movement of history toward the perfect State seems to have been omitted from the discussion. Here the hero is the founder of the State. But as such he has the same rights and the same role as the *great man.* He is not constrained by morality, neither reflective morality nor the other morality (i.e., ethics), which is the concrete form of life:

---

lecture notes. We can therefore be certain that it accurately expresses his thought, although we cannot rely on the precise wording of this manuscript because it was not prepared for publication. [I have translated Weil's French directly, and in addition to the pages from the Lasson edition, provided by Weil, I give the pages from the most widely used English translation, *The Philosophy of History,* trans. J. Sibree (1899; reprint, New York, 1956). TRANS.]

15. Ibid., Lasson 65; Sibree 25.
16. Ibid., Lasson 63; Sibree 23.
17. Ibid., Lasson 68; Sibree 31.

When there is only a state of nature, a state of generalized violence, the idea [of organized freedom] establishes against it [the
state of nature] a right of heroes. (*PhR* §93, 93; Knox, 67)[18]

There can no longer be any heroes in a State. They live only
when an uncivilized [*ungebildet*] state of affairs prevails . . . The
heroes who founded States . . . admittedly did not do this pur-
suant to a recognized right, and their actions still appear to have
been the result of their particular will. But as the higher right
of the idea against nature, this heroic coercion is in accord with
right, for goodness can achieve virtually nothing against the
violence of nature. (*PhR* add. to §93, 93; Knox, 245)[19]

It is true that when civilization attains a more fully developed stage
in the State, only one virtue is demanded of the citizen, decency [*hon-
nêteté*]. Virtue in the strict sense, classical virtue [*virtus*], would now
be out of place since it only appears in *conflicts,* which do not occur
(except as rare exceptions or in an imaginary form) in organized life:
"the form of virtue as such appears more in the uncivilized stage of
societies and communities, since here the ethical [*das Sittliche*] and its
realization are more [the result of] a personal whim or the particular
and genial nature of an individual" (PhR §150, 161; Knox, 108).[20]

But is the hero only present while States are being founded, be-

18. "Entweder ist ein sittliches Dasein in Familie oder Staat schon gesetzt, gegen
welche jene Natürlichkeit eine Gewalttätigkeit ist, oder es ist nur ein Naturzustand,
—Zustand der Gewalt überhaupt vorhanden, so begründet die Idee gegen diesen
ein *Heroenrecht.*" [In more recent editions of *PhR* this last word reads "Herrenrecht"
(master right). TRANS.]

19. "Im Staat kann es keine Heroen mehr geben: diese kommen nur im ungebildeten Zustande vor . . . Die Heroen, die Staaten stifteten . . . haben dieses freilich
nicht als anerkanntes Recht getan, und diese Handlungen erscheinen noch als ihr
besonderer Wille; aber als das höhere Recht der Idee gegen die Natürlichkeit ist
dieser Zwang der Heroen ein rechtlicher; denn in der Güte läßt sich gegen die Gewalt der Natur wenig ausrichten."

20. "Im ungebildeten Zustande der Gesellschaft und des Gemeinwesens kommt
deswegen mehr die Form der Tugend als solcher vor, weil hier das Sittliche und
dessen Verwirklichung mehr ein individuelles Belieben und eine eigentümliche ge-
niale Natur des Individuums ist."

fore the beginning of history proper? "It is the absolute right of the idea to come into existence in norms of law and objective institutions . . . whether the form of its realization appears as divine legislation and divine gift or as violence and injustice—this right is the right of heroes to found states" (*PhR* §350, 348–49; Knox, 219).[21] To found States? But what is the founding of a State? What is it if not the realization of a new principle of organization, the creation of "norms of law and objective institutions," if not the "extremely turbulent play of passions, interests, competing ends, natural talents and virtues, violence, wrongs and vice, as well as external chance" discussed above.[22] How does the movement of history, this struggle of principles embodied in different peoples, make any progress if not by marching behind the standard of *great men*? And are these great men not in effect the heroes of the age of well-constituted States? Hegel's answer leaves no room for doubt:

> At the head of all actions, which therefore includes those important for universal history, can be found individuals, who are able to act by virtue of their being subjectivities, that realize the substantial. As they are these living forms and forces [*Lebendigkeiten*] of the substantial activity of the world spirit and are therefore immediately identical with that activity, it remains concealed from them and is not [for them] an aim or object. (*PhR* §348, 347–48; Knox, 218)[23]

The great man is therefore equivalent to the hero of modern times. It is he who realizes the new principle—losing his life or freedom in

21. "In gesetzlichen Bestimmungen und in objektiven Institutionen . . . hervorzutreten, ist das absolute Recht der Idee, es sei, daß die Form dieser ihrer Verwirklichung als göttliche Gesetzgebung und Wohltat, oder als Gewalt und Unrecht erscheine;—dies Recht ist das *Heroenrecht* zur Stiftung von Staaten."

22. See the text cited in n. 9, 81, above.

23. "An der Spitze aller Handlungen, somit auch der welthistorischen, stehen *Individuen* als die das Substantielle verwirklichenden Subjektivitäten. Als diesen Lebendigkeiten der substantiellen Tat des Weltgeistes und so unmittelbar identisch mit derselben, ist sie ihnen selbst verborgen und nicht Objekt und Zweck."

the process—by dint of his passion and violence, by war.[24] The state of nature has not yet been annulled, history has not yet come to an end, hero and action are still central to the unfurling of events in the world.

*  *  *

Are we then dealing with a history of great men, a conception comparable to that of Carlyle (and his innumerable successors)? Not at all. The great man is great because he realizes what is *objectively,* according to the rational concept of freedom, the stage above him in development. He is a genius, that is, an incomprehensible phenome-

24. It is clear that Hegel was thinking above all of Napoleon; see the references to him in *Philosophie der Weltgeschichte,* vol. 4, *Die Germanische Welt,* 930 ff., and esp. 78; and on the role and the tragedy of great men in general see ibid., 74 ff. In another place the term *hero* is applied to the great men of historical ages who "do not find their goals and their vocation in a tranquil and ordered system, in the sanctified course of affairs. Their justification is not to be found in the existing state of affairs but is drawn from a different source. From the hidden spirit, which wages war on the present, which is still underground, which has not yet evolved into a concrete existence [*Dasein*], and which strives to emerge" (ibid., 75). Meanwhile war is, strictly speaking, the arena of heroism. "The moral aspect [*Moment*] of war, which is not to be regarded as an absolute evil and as a purely external accident," is to be found in the sacrifice of the finite, of life and property. It is in this sacrifice that the perishable is *posited* and desired as perishable by freedom, by negativity. Hegel quotes his article on *Natural Law:* "War has the higher significance that by means of it . . . ethical health is preserved from being fixed in finite determinations, just as the movement of the winds preserves the ocean from the corruption that permanent calm would bring about in it, in the same way in nations a durable, or even perpetual peace (would bring about corruption)" (*PhR* §324, 332–33; Knox, 210). This recalls the thesis of the *Phenomenology,* whereby only those who confront death come to realize the negativity of freedom in themselves. Here, at this initial stage of human development, the individual is the nation organized as a State. But this is only a memory. Later in the same paragraph Hegel says that all this "is *only* [Hegel's italics] a philosophical idea, or, to use another common expression, a justification by Providence, and that actual wars require some other justification." The use of the words "philosophical idea" in a pejorative sense, preceded by "only," is striking and shows that Hegel did not find this philosophical justification (we would call it "moralistic" or "idealistic") to be sufficient, although this did not lead him to make his true thesis explicit; it is only hinted at implicitly in the later sections of the book. Students of Hegel will have to reconstruct it.

non only for those who do not perceive his objective role and who are content with a psychological analysis of man, not according to his greatness, but according to his shared humanity.[25]

But this remark alone does not go far enough to illustrate fully how the great man's action, the reason or cause that leads "the peoples to rally around his standard," actually works. We should now consider the second part of Hegel's answer, to which I made reference above. We shall have to examine the men who follow the great man, and no longer the great man himself, who guides them because he realizes their unconscious and unspoken aspirations. In order to do this we must backtrack somewhat and look at the *Philosophy of Right* from a point of view that offers us the only permissible way to definitively resolve the problem at hand: is the modern State as it is effectively realized by Prussia the perfect form of the State, and if not (the preceding texts have already shown that this is indeed the case), what could replace it? Are we entering a new era in which the only struggles will be between modern States all of which have an identical form, or is it the form of the State itself that is at stake?

The central thread running through history is the realization of freedom in an organization that gives satisfaction to all men. But what is a man? The discussion so far has revolved around great men, heroes. It has also been about the different groups making up society, the functions that, taken together, form the State, and about *Man,* about the negativity and the freedom that are the essence of *Man.* It has not been about man in the current sense of the word, about man as the basic element of any group, for whom and by whom freedom is realized. We have only been exposed to one trait, the essential one in Hegel's eyes: that man is neither isolated nor isolable, that he *is* whatever he *does* in society; and since men do not all do the same things,

25. See *PhR* §124, 121; Knox, 84, where Hegel quotes the following passage from the *Phenomenology:* "This is the view of those valet psychologists 'for whom there are no heroes, not because there are no heroes, but because these psychologists are only valets'" (*Phänomenologie des Geistes* [1807], ed. G. Lasson, 2d ed. [Leipzig, 1921], 616; *Hegel's Phenomenology of Spirit,* trans. A. V. Miller [Oxford, 1977], 404).

they are not equal either. There is equality in the abstract sense, certainly, that of private persons and equality before the law:

> It is part of the education of spirit [*Bildung*], of thought as the consciousness of the individual in the form of the universal, that *I* am conceived as a universal person, in which all are identical. Man has value [*gilt*] because he is a man, not because he is a Jew, a Catholic, a Protestant, a German, an Italian, etc. This consciousness that holds thought to be of value [*gilt*] is of infinite importance, is deficient only when it takes on a fixed form so as to oppose itself to the concrete life of the State, for instance, as cosmopolitanism. (*PhR* §209, 207; Knox, 209)[26]

There is equality, then, but an equality that does not deny structural differences, that manifests itself and becomes a concrete reality through the differentiation of its organization. The State is a circle made up of circles,

> and in the State no one of its moments must [*soll*] appear as an unorganized mass. The many, as [the total group] of isolated parts, what we are pleased to think of as the people, are of course a unity, but only as a mass, a formless mass whose movement and activity could only be elementary, irrational, wild and terrifying . . . The representation that dissolves these communities as they now exist in these circles into a mass of individuals again as soon as they enter the realm of politics, that is, from the point of view of the highest concrete universality, precisely separates as it does so civil from political life and founds the latter on air, so to speak, since its basis would not then be a foundation that was solid and justified in and for itself, but only

26. "Es gehört der Bildung, dem *Denken* als Bewußtsein des Einzelnen in Form der Allgemeinheit, daß Ich als *allgemeine* Person aufgefaßt werde, worin *Alle* identisch sind. Der *Mensch gilt so, weil er Mensch ist,* nicht weil er Jude, Katholik, Protestant, Deutscher, Italiener, u.s.f. ist. Dies Bewußtsein, dem der *Gedanke* gilt, ist von unendlicher Wichtigkeit, — nur dann mangelhaft, wenn es etwa als *Kosmopolitismus* sich dazu fixiert, dem konkreten Staatsleben gegenüberzustehen."

the abstract individuality of caprice and opinion, and therefore founded on the accidental. (*PhR* §303, 313–14; Knox, 198)[27]

The political (in the narrow sense) consequences of this thesis are not relevant here (I have said that for Hegel formal democracy, that of direct elections, does not represent the height of political wisdom); rather we are interested in what implications it has for men in society: equality, which is an incontestable and indubitable right because it is the foundation of right, does not exhaust the political concept of man.

But there does exist a definition of man in society that is more generally applicable. Or to be more accurate, it is in society that the possibility of defining man can be found: "On the level of needs, it [the object of the inquiry] is the concrete reality of the *representation* that we call man. It is therefore only here, and strictly speaking here and here alone, that man is considered in this sense" (*PhR* §190, 195; Knox, 127).[28]

What is *generally* meant when one speaks of man, the way he is *generally* "represented," is defined from the standpoint of needs, or more precisely, from the standpoint of those needs that are not purely animal:

> An animal has a limited range of ways and means for satisfying its needs, which are equally limited. Even in his similar depen-

27. "Der Staat aber ist wesentlich eine Organisation von solchen Gliedern, die *für sich Kreise* sind, und in ihm soll sich kein Moment als eine unorganische Menge zeigen. *Die Vielen* als Einzelne, was man gerne unter Volk versteht, sind wohl ein *Zusammen,* aber nur als die *Menge,* — eine formlose Masse, deren Bewegung und Tun eben damit nur elementarisch, vernunftlos, wild und fürchterlich wäre . . . Die Vorstellung, welche die in jenen Kreisen schon vorhandenen Gemeinwesen, wo sie ins Politische, d.i. in den Standpunkt der *höchsten konkreten Allgemeinheit* eintreten, wieder in eine Menge von Individuen auflöst, hält eben damit das bürgerliche und das politische Leben voneinander getrennt, und stellt dieses sozusagen, in die Luft, da seine Basis nur die abstrakte Einzelheit der Willkür und Meinung, somit das Zufällige, nicht eine an und für sich *feste* und *berechtige* Grundlage sein würde."

28. "Auf dem Standpunkte der Bedürfniße ist es das Konkretum *der Vorstellung,* das man *Mensch* nennt; es ist also erst hier und auch eigentlich nur hier vom *Menschen* in diesem Sinne die Rede."

dence man shows his transcendence [*Hinausgehen*] of it and his universality, first, by the multiplication of needs and means and, second, by the division and differentiation of concrete need into various parts and separate aspects that make up different particularized and so more abstract needs. (Ibid.) [29]

Man develops historical needs, social needs, which are opposed to and soon eclipse natural needs. As a result, he finds himself confronted with a need that belongs to him, a necessity that he has created himself. He remains unaware of this, and so the need appears to be something external, a product of chance, but a chance that is internal, his own arbitrary decision.[30]

Man is therefore a being that has needs, but needs that are also his own product in and for society [*oeuvre sociale*], just as the means to satisfy them are equally produced by his labor. It is true that this definition does not yet provide the *concept* of man but only its *representation*. Yet it is the theoretical weakness of this definition that makes it so useful for our purposes, since we are seeking to discover how man, the man of ordinary and everyday life, not the great man or the hero,

29. "Das *Tier* hat einen beschränkten Kreis von Mitteln und Weisen der Befriedigung seiner gleichfalls beschränkten Bedürfnisse. Der *Mensch* beweist auch in dieser Abhängigkeit zugleich sein Hinausgehen über dieselbe und seine Allgemeinheit, zunächst durch die *Vervielfältigung* der Bedürfnisse und Mittel, und dann durch *Zerlegung* und *Unterscheidung* des konkreten Bedürfnisses in einzelne Teile und Seiten, welche verschiedene *partikularisierte,* damit *abstraktere* Bedürfnisse werden."

30. The paragraph of which I am giving a truncated summary follows: "Indem im gesellschaftlichen Bedürfnisse, als der Verknüpfung vom unmittelbaren oder natürlichen und vom geistigen Bedürfnisse der *Vorstellung,* das letztere sich als das Allgemeine zum Überwiegenden macht, so liegt in diesem gesellschaftlichen Momente die Seite der *Befreiung,* daß die strenge Naturnotwendigkeit des Bedürfnisses versteckt wird, und der Mensch sich zu *seiner,* und zwar einer allgemeinen *Meinung* und einer nur selbstgemachten Notwendigkeit statt nur zu äußerlicher, zu innerer Zufälligkeit, zur *Willkür,* verhält" [Since in social needs, as the conjunction of immediate or natural needs with mental needs arising from ideas, it is needs of the latter type that, because of their universality, make themselves preponderant, this social moment has in it the aspect of liberation, so that the strict natural necessity of need is covered over and man is concerned with *his own* opinion, indeed with a *universal* opinion, and a necessity of his own making alone, instead of with an external necessity, inner contingency, and *caprice*] (*PhR* §194, 196–97; Knox, 128).

behaves. It is this man, as he appears to himself in the representation he forms of himself, who must be reconciled with himself. He *must* be reconciled; *is* he in fact? And does *Hegel's account* claim that he is?

❋ ❋ ❋

In one of the quotations cited above a term is employed to which we paid no attention at the time, namely, *populace*,[31] meaning the mass of people who "presuppose ill will or insufficiently good will on the part of the government," who represent "the point of view of the negative." The time has come for us to ask who these people are, what the populace is, where it comes from, and what its role is. For one thing must be clear by now: the Hegelian State is conceived in such a way as to give satisfaction to *all* rational individuals. If a single group in it remains *essentially* unsatisfied, then the State is a failure. In the Hegelian State it is intolerable that parties and groups still exist that are in conflict over vital issues.

> It is among the most widespread but extremely dangerous preju-
> dices to present the Estates [*Stände*] principally as being in oppo-
> sition to the government . . . If it [i.e., the opposition] was not
> only a surface phenomenon, when it appeared, but became sub-
> stantial opposition, then the State would have begun to perish.
> (*PhR* §302, 312; Knox, 197)[32]

31. See ch. 4, n. 17, and the text preceding the note. In order to understand the special meaning of the conception of populace *(Pöbel)* as Hegel develops it, it is useful to compare it with the Kantian notion. "The section [of the nation] that is excluded from the laws (the uncivilized mob from among the people) is called the populace *(vulgus)*, whose illegal gatherings represent the act of fomenting faction *(agere per turbas)*, which excludes it from enjoying the status of citizen in the State" (*Anthropologie in pragmatischer Hinsicht,* in *Werke,* ed. E. Cassirer [Berlin, 1912–18], 8:204 ff.). For Kant the problem is therefore neither historical nor political but purely moral. It is a question of obeying the laws of the State. He does not ask about the provenance, meaning, or consequences of disobedience. He is satisfied simply to pass judgment. In other words, Kant is interested in the individual, who does not have the *right* to rebel, not in the State, which must take into account the *possibility* of rebellion.

32. "[W]eil es zu den häufigen, aber höchst gefährlichen Vorurteilen gehört,

It is precisely such a substantial opposition that makes its appearance here: there exist people who *deny* the State, who are therefore striving to destroy it. How can this be explained? How can *man,* man as he conceives himself existing in society, man as he grasps himself in representation, this same man of whom we have just been speaking, refuse the State? Why does he do so? Is it his incorrigible malice? His irresponsible and arbitrary opinions? Or, on the contrary, is it society itself that produces men who have no stake in it, who cannot find their rational satisfaction, that is, the recognition of their infinite value in it, and cannot do so because, rationally speaking, it is not in fact to be found there?

＊ ＊ ＊

These are the very questions asked by Hegel himself, and as long as we pay close attention to what he actually says they will not need any further interpretation. In society man performs labor. Acting in his own private interest in this way, he also acts in the interest of everyone. Property, in the sense that it is an immediate expression of personal will, loses whatever importance it previously possessed once it becomes part of a developed organization, whereupon it gives way to *wealth:* the foundation of the family and its concrete morality, in which individual desire is transformed into a concern for the common good. It is in terms of wealth that the family "has the existence of its substantial personality" (*PhR* §169, 175; Knox, 116).[33] In the same way that the family gets assimilated into civil society, as history progresses the function of family wealth is transformed as soon as a more developed organization allows for the establishment and

---

Stände hauptsächlich im Gesichtspunkte des *Gegensatzes* gegen die Regierung . . . vorzustellen . . . Wenn er, insofern er seine Erscheinung hat, nicht bloß die Oberfläche beträfe, sondern wirklich ein substantieller Gegensatz würde, so wäre der Staat in seinem Untergange begriffen."

33. "Die Familie hat als Person ihre äußerliche Realität in einem *Eigentum,* in dem sie das dasein ihrer substantiellen Persönlichkeit nur als in einem *Vermögen* hat." See also §170.

preservation of *social wealth*. In the same way that an individual in an advanced society labors in the interest of all while imagining that he is pursuing his personal interest, his individual wealth is ultimately revealed to be participation in the propagation of universal wealth.

> The necessity constituted by the total intertwinement resulting from everyone's interdependence now presents itself to each person as the universal and permanent wealth that contains the possibility for him to participate in it by virtue of his education and skill in order to be assured of his subsistence; in the same way this benefit accruing to the individual through his labor maintains and increases the universal wealth. (*PhR* §199, 199–200; Knox, 130) [34]

But this participation in the general wealth is dependent on certain conditions. It is itself mediated, whether by capital, an "immediate and proper basis," [35] or by "education and skill," the capacities and the professional training, which vary according to the individual, the external conditions, and also according to the differences between families' respective levels of wealth.[36]

---

34. "Diese Notwendigkeit, die in der allseitigen Verschlingung der Abhängigkeit aller liegt, ist nunmehr für jeden das *allgemeine, bleibende Vermögen,* das für ihn die Möglichkeit enthält, durch seine Bildung und Geschicklichkeit daran teilzunehmen, um für seine Subsistenz gesichert zu sein,—so wie dieser durch seine Arbeit vermittelte Erwerb das allgemeine Vermögen erhält und vermehrt."

35. The appearance of the term *immediate* in connection with the description of wealth as capital is significant because for Hegel private capital does not constitute a perfectly mediated element within society. This can only be realized by *social* capital and, in the final analysis, social labor [*le travail social*].

36. "Die *Möglichkeit* der *Teilnahme* an dem allgemeinen Vermögen, das *besondere* Vermögen, ist aber *bedingt,* teils durch eine unmittelbare eigene Grundlage (Kapital), teils durch die Geschicklichkeit, welche ihrerseits wieder selbst durch jenes, dann aber durch die zufälligen Umstände bedingt ist, deren mannigfaltigkeit die *Verschiedenheit* in der *Entwicklung* der schon *für sich ungleichen* natürlichen körperlichen und geistigen Anlagen hervorbringt,—eine Verschiedenheit, die in dieser Sphäre der besonderheit nach allen Richtungen und von allen Stufen sich hervortut und mit der übrigen Zufälligkeit und Willkür die *Ungleichheit* des Vermögens und der *Geschicklichkeiten* der Individuen zur notwendigen Folge hat" [The possibility of participating in the universal wealth, that is, his particular wealth, is determined, however,

Hegel has often been lauded for seeing that the essence of modern man's existence in society lay in labor. But almost as often this praise has been followed by the caveat that he only saw labor as an abstract concept and neglected its concrete and historical forms. If this critique is justified, and even then only to a certain degree, in the case of the *Phenomenology of Spirit,* it is completely groundless when extended to the *Philosophy of Right.* Although he only noted them in passing, nevertheless Hegel has given us a correct and comprehensive picture of the characteristic traits of modern social labor.

The most important thing to understand in this connection is that not only does Hegel distinguish between the social estates [*états sociaux*] —farmers, civil servants, and tradespersons, the latter further subdivided into artisans, manufacturers, and retailers—a distinction already well established in Hegel's day and approaching obsolescence even then; not only does he conceive money to be the universal commodity, which goes without saying for someone who had read Adam Smith, J.-B. Say, and Ricardo; but he sees and says clearly what the modern division of labor means for the individual's conditions of existence:

> The labor of the individual is simplified by division, and consequently the skill [of the individual] in his abstract labor and the quantity of his production grow. At the same time, this abstraction of skill and means renders the dependence and mutual relations [*Wechselbeziehung*] of men in the satisfaction of their other needs more complete, to the point of [making it] an absolute necessity. Furthermore, the abstraction of the way in which something is produced makes labor more and more mechanical and ultimately makes it possible for man to step aside [from

partly by his direct ownership of resources (his capital) and partly by his skill; this in turn is determined by his resources but also by accidental circumstances whose multiplicity introduces differences in the development of natural, bodily, and mental abilities, which were already dissimilar in themselves, differences that in this sphere of particularity accentuate themselves in every direction and on every level and that, together with the contingency and arbitrariness, have as their necessary consequence the inequality of individual wealth and skills] (*PhR* §200, 200; Knox 130).

his labor] and for the machine to replace him. (*PhR* §198, 199; Knox, 129) [37]

What is striking about this text is its insistence on the increasingly *abstract* character of labor broken down into separate tasks. It is no longer the whole person who is performing it (in which case Hegel would call it concrete) but only an increasingly limited, increasingly specialized, increasingly mechanical portion of his faculties and his knowledge. When the machine has replaced man, he finds himself faced with a hostile form of life that has all the characteristics of pure and implacable [*totale*] necessity: the contrary of freedom.

For a philosopher devoted to the freedom of each and every person these insights had profound implications, but Hegel is not content simply to leave them as they stand. To be sure, he expresses himself prudently and with a certain veiled indirectness. Is this because he wished to avoid trouble? Or because he thought that the problem was purely theoretical and of no real concern to him, since he was living in a country that had no industry and could therefore observe with utter detachment what was taking place (or, more precisely, was beginning to take place) abroad? Such questions are irrelevant. What *is* certain is that he was fully aware of what the new mode of labor meant *for man* and so was prepared to take his analysis a step further.

I have already remarked that from the Hegelian point of view *human* need represents the first stage in being freed from the bonds of nature and that *desire* and its satisfaction in labor give man a feeling of his freedom since he is no longer dependent on natural need but on his own arbitrary decision [*arbitraire*]. This phrase *arbitrary decision* should

---

37. "Das Arbeiten des Einzelnen wird durch die Teilung *einfacher* und hierdurch die Geschicklichkeit in seiner abstrakten Arbeit, sowie die Menge seiner Produktion grösser. Zugleich vervollständigt diese Abstraktion der Geschicklichkeit und des Mittels die *Abhängigkeit* und die *Wechselbeziehung* der Menschen für die Befriedigung der übrigen Bedürfnisse zur gänzlichen Notwendigkeit. Die Abstraktion des Produzierens macht das Arbeiten ferner immermehr *mechanisch* und damit am Ende fähig, daß der Mensch davon wegtreten und an seine Stelle die *Maschine* eintreten lassen kann."

give us pause. It never appears (no more than the terms *representation, chance,* and *opinion,* which are also present in this paragraph)³⁸ without the implication that freedom and reason have not yet been attained. Hegel does not rely on the intelligence of his readers to draw the right conclusion; he draws it himself in a passage whose force can be fully appreciated only now:

> This liberation is purely formal . . . When the state of society tends toward the indeterminate multiplication and specification of needs, means, and pleasures . . . [i.e., toward] luxury, this entails an equally infinite increase in dependence and want [*Not*], which have to struggle with a matter that offers an infinite resistance, namely, external means that have the special character of being the property of free will, [which have to struggle with] something absolutely unyielding. (*PhR* §195, 197–98; Knox, 128)³⁹

What this amounts to is that while on the one hand dividends, the total stock of the means of production and general wealth, all increase, on the other, the level of dependency of men (those who do not own anything) grows at exactly the same rate and will do so indefinitely. And this dependency is based on the fact that the means of production are in the hands of one group of individuals; access to these means of production depends on the free will of these persons; and ultimately modern society produces men who, even if they want to, cannot participate in social wealth by the only legitimate route, by their freely given labor.

At this point the meaning of another passage cited above becomes clear. In the State "no one of its moments must [*doit*] appear as an un-

---

38. See n. 29 and the text that follows it.
39. "Diese Befreiung ist *formell* . . . Die Richtung des gesellschaftlichen Zustandes auf die unbestimmte vervielfältigung und Spezifizierung der Bedürfnisse, Mittel und Genüsse . . . der *Luxus*—ist eine ebenso unendliche Vermehrung der Abhängigkeit und *Not,* welche es mit einer den unendlichen Widerstand leistenden Materie, nämlich mit äußeren Mitteln von der besonderen Art, Eigentum des freien Willens zu sein, dem absolut Harten, zu tun hat."

organized mass."⁴⁰ The word *must* [*doit*] needs to be stressed here, for is it not perfectly unacceptable from the Hegelian point of view for any *have to* or *duty* [*devoir*]⁴¹ to still need to be applied to the State? Is the State not precisely the realized organization of freedom, the reality of reason that has transcended morality with its rules that we are free to obey or disobey? The simple word *must* [*doit*] seems to indicate that the State is not as perfect as it *ought* to be [*devrait être*], that if it is not totally organized, in other words, if there are still individuals in it who are nothing but a "rabble" and an inorganic "mass," then to this degree the State has not been realized.

Some readers will be led to protest that I rely rather heavily on one word to make definitive conclusions about Hegel's attitude toward the modern State. This objection would be valid if our interpretation were not confirmed by the fully developed theory of society to be found in the rest of Hegel's work. For one thing, the State has the unquestionable right and duty to intervene in the economy, in the administration of the general wealth. "The different interests of producers and consumers may come into conflict with each other; and if it is true that in general a just balance is automatically produced, still their adjustment also requires a regulation that is superior to both and consciously undertaken" (*PhR* §236, 228; Knox, 147).⁴² This intervention on the part of the State—because it is the State that stands above the particular interests of consumers and producers and acts con-

---

40. See above, n. 27.

41. [The infinitive *devoir*, meaning "to have to," picks up the *doit*, or "must," of the previous line (which roughly translates the German *sollen* in the original). It is equally a noun, in which form it means "duty," referring forward to "la morale" in the following line, which for Hegel means primarily Kantian ethics, with its reliance on duty, rules, and the separation of the empirical from the moral. The next line contains yet another form of the verb *devoir*, the conditional in the third-person singular, *devrait*, "ought to." TRANS.]

42. "Die verschiedenen Interessen der Produzenten und Konsumenten können in Kollision miteinander kommen, und wenn sich zwar das richtige Verhältnis *im ganzen* von selbst herstellt, so bedarf die Ausgleichung auch einer über beiden stehenden mit Bewußtsein vorgenommenen Regulierung . . . um die gefährlichen Zuckungen und die Dauer des Zwischenraumes, in welchem sich die Kollisionen auf dem Wege bewußtloser Notwendigkeit ausgleichen sollen, abzukürzen und zu mildern."

sciously—is necessary for two reasons: first, international economic relations and the dependence of the national economy on the international market present problems of such difficulty and complexity that the egotism of individuals is inadequate for their comprehension or their solution, but above all—and the Hegelian concern for satisfaction makes itself felt here—the government must act "to abbreviate and diminish the spasmodic movements and length of time in which conflicts are resolved by means of unconscious necessity" (ibid.). The government cannot rely on economic forces alone to bring an end to economic crises. Unconscious necessity (and in Hegel this term denotes nature: the laws of the economy act on the individual in the same way as the laws of nature) must be conquered by reason in the interests of, and by, free and conscious action. The economy is subordinate to the State; political economy is a necessity.

Does this mean that Hegel advocates autarchy and the maximum degree of State intervention to defend the citizens' interests? If the answer is yes, this would only redound to Hegel's credit. Once again, his analysis of existing conditions has provided an accurate description of how modern States behave, whether one approves of these practices or not. But this is not all, I feel. Hegel is concerned above all with the historical emergence of this so-called *rabble, mass,* or *populace* that regards the State *from the point of view of the negative* and thus constitutes a *party* in the proper sense of the word, an opposition based not on small-scale technical differences over administration or purely personal conflicts but on the foundation of the State itself. And the central point of Hegel's analysis is that the populace as an oppositional entity is necessarily created by society itself.

> Circumstances due to chance, physical conditions, caused by external relations, can reduce individuals to poverty, a state that still leaves them with the needs of civil society and that, after taking the natural means of acquisition and annulled the bonds of the family in the wider sense of clan, deprives them more or less of all the advantages of society, of the opportunity to acquire a skill or education of any kind, and equally deprives them of justice, health care, and often even the consolations of

religion, and so on. For the *poor,* the universal government takes the place of the family with respect not only to their immediate destitution but also to any characteristic aversion to work, malignity, and the other vices that have their origin in their present situation and their sense of wrong. (*PhR* §241, 230–31; Knox, 148)[43]

When the standard of living of a large mass of people falls below a certain level of subsistence, which is regulated automatically as the subsistence necessary for a member of the society, and with it the loss of the sense of right, of honesty, and of honor that comes from maintaining oneself by one's own activity and labor, the result is the production of the *populace,* a production that, for its part, leads to the greater ease with which disproportionate wealth gets concentrated in a few hands. (*PhR* §244, 232; Knox, 150)[44]

Or to put Hegel's comments in a more contemporary form: the sphere of social labor's living under the regime of the private appropriation of the means of production leads to the creation of the proletariat, whose existence is necessary for the accumulation of this productive wealth:

43. "Aber ebenso als die Willkür können zufallige, physische und in der äußeren Verhältnissen liegende Umstände Individuen zur *Armut* herunterbringen, einem Zustande, der ihnen die Bedürfnisse der bürgerlichen Gesellschaft läßt, und der—indem sie ihnen zugleich die natürlichen Erwerbsmittel entzogen und das weitere Band der Familie als eines Stammes aufhebt,—dagegen sie aller Vorteile der Gesellschaft, Erwerbsfähigkeit von Geschicklichkeiten und Bildung überhaupt, auch der Rechtspflege, Gesundheitssorge, selbst oft des Trostes der Religion usf. mehr oder weniger verlustig macht. Die allgemeine macht übernimmt die Stelle der Familie bei den *Armen* ebensosehr in Rücksicht ihres unmittelbaren Mangels als der Gesinnung der Arbeitsscheu, Bösartigkeit und der weiteren Laster, die als solcher Lage und dem Gefühl ihres Unrechts entspringen."

44. "Das Herabsinken einer großen Masse unter das Maß einer gewissen Subsistenzweise, die sich von selbst als die für ein Mitglied der Gesellschaft notwendige reguliert,—und damit zum Verluste des Gefühls des Rechts, der Rechtlichkeit und der Ehre, durch eigene Tätigkeit und Arbeit zu bestehen,—bringt die Erzeugung des *Pöbels* hervor, die hinwiederum zugleich die größere Leichtigkeit, unverhältnismäßige Reichtümer in wenige Hände zu konzentrieren, mit sich führt."

> If civil society is operating without any impediment, it is con-
> tinually increasing its domestic population and industry . . .
> As the amassing of wealth increases on one side, so, to the
> same degree, does the greater specification and limitation of
> any particular form of labor on the other, and, as a result, the
> dependence and destitution of the class tied to work of that
> sort, which further entails the inability to experience the other
> capacities and in particular the spiritual advantages of civil
> society and to enjoy them. (*PhR* §243, 232; Knox, 149)[45]

It is not because of malice that the proletariat has no part in the State
and the civilization, it is not because of in-born prejudices that it has
no homeland, lacks a sense of honor, and refuses to adhere to the
laws of morality. Society is constituted in such a way that it necessarily produces this evil, and it will persist as long as the State will
not or cannot create a rational organization whose overriding aim is
the realization of freedom and the recognition of all by all. "Against
nature no one can claim a right. But in the social State any deficiency
straight away takes the form of a wrong done to one class by another"
(*PhR* add. to §244; Knox, 277).[46]

It is at this point that we come to the heart of the Hegelian conception of the State. This wrong that is committed by society — whose

45. "Wenn die bürgerliche Gesellschaft sich in ungehinderter Wirksamkeit be-
findet, so ist sie innerhalb ihrer selbst in *fortschreitender* Bevölkerung und Industrie
begriffen . . . [Es] vermehrt sich die *Anhäufung der Reichtümer* . . . auf der einen Seite,
wie auf der anderen Seite die *Vereinzelung* und *Beschränktheit* der besonderen Arbeit
und damit die *Abhängigkeit* und *Not* der an diese Arbeit gebundenen Klasse, womit
die Unfähigkeit der Empfindung und des Genusses der weiteren Fähigkeiten [In
some editions this reads "Freiheiten" (freedoms). TRANS.] und besonders der geistigen Vorteile der bürgerlichen Gesellschaft zusammenhängt." It is interesting to
note the use of the term *class* in the sense that will become standard with Marx; see
also the following note.

46. "Gegen die Natur kann kein Mensch ein Recht behaupten; aber im Zustande
der Gesellschaft gewinnt der Mangel sogleich die Form eines Unrechts, was dieser
oder jener Klasse angetan wird." This addition simply expresses in a more striking
way what is said in §241 (see above, n. 43) of the text published by Hegel. There
too the *wrong* is said to be *poverty*.

essential constitution is that of a pseudonatural entity, that is, unconscious necessity—and is responsible for the *negativity* of the *populace*
cannot be rectified by it for the precise reason that society did not
want this wrong since as a pseudonatural entity it does not *want,* is
unable to *want,* and because it is irrational, which amounts to the
same thing. As pseudonature it can only continue as it began; it is
inevitable that it will produce *alienated* man, lacking morality, faith,
education, skill, honor, and family, a man who ceases to be a free
citizen from the moment he is forced to sell all of his time, for "by
the alienation [*Veräußerung*] of the totality of my time, as made concrete in my labor, and the totality of my production, I would be
making another's property by means of my substantial concrete time,
my universal activity and reality [effective reality, *Wirklichkeit*], and
my person" (*PhR* §67, 69; Knox, 54). In addition, as if he was afraid
that he might not be understood, Hegel recalls the thesis of his *Logic,*
"The totality of the expressions of a power is that power itself."[47]

Society has brought the populace into existence. It is not responsible for it since it did not want it to exist—it is not capable of wanting. But this means that it is equally incapable of finding a remedy
for the populace's ills and that within its own sphere it does not even
possess the potential to do so since it cannot go beyond benevolence
or good will. Not only is good will an inadequate resource for a State,
which as a rational organization must keep itself independent of the
feelings and opinions of its citizens as it is acting to realize its ends,[48]
but this good will only serves to aggravate the evil it is seeking to
combat.

> If one imposed this burden directly on the class of the rich
> or if there existed some other publicly owned resource (well-

47. "Durch die Veräußerung meiner ganzen durch die Arbeit konkreten Zeit
und der Totalität meiner Produktion würde ich das Substantielle derselben, meine
*allgemeine* Tätigkeit und Wirklichkeit, meine Persönlichkeit zum Eigentum eines
anderen machen . . . Die *Totalität* der Äußerungen einer Kraft selbst." The man who
is subject to the *necessity* of economic mechanisms therefore sells not his labor but
his labor power.

48. See the critique of the role that the moral convictions and attitudes of the
citizens in different constitutions play in Montesquieu's theory in *PhR* §273.

endowed hospitals, foundations, convents) to serve to directly maintain the masses presently threatened with poverty at a suitably comfortable standard of living, the subsistence of those in need would be assured without being the result of their labor, and this would violate the principle of civil society and the feeling its individual members have of their independence and honor. Or their subsistence could be made the result of their labor (of being given the chance to work) and in this event the volume of goods produced would be increased, the same volume whose abundance, together with a lack of a corresponding number of consumers who are also producers themselves, was the very cause of the problem and that either solution only makes worse. It appears, then, that with its surplus wealth bourgeois society is not rich enough; that is, its own particular resources are insufficient to do much to combat excessive poverty and the creation of the populace. (*PhR* §245, 232–33; Knox, 150)[49]

There is no need to insist on the wealth of insight to be found in this text. Beginning with the refusal of a benevolence that would be the contrary of what any man has the right to demand, namely, the recognition of his value as a citizen-producer, Hegel concludes with an analysis of the phenomenon of what has since been called the crisis of overproduction, or more accurately, the crisis of underconsumption.

49. "Wird der reicheren Klasse die direkte Last aufgelegt, oder es wären in anderem öffentlichen Eigentum (reichen Hospitälern, Stiftungen, Klöstern) die direkten Mittel vorhanden, die der Armut zugehende Masse auf dem Stande ihrer ordentlichen Lebensweise zu erhalten, so würde die Subsistenz der Bedürftigen gesichert, ohne durch die Arbeit vermittelt zu sein, was gegen das Prinzip der bürgerlichen Gesellschaft und des Gefühls ihrer Individuen von ihrer Selbstständigkeit und Ehre wäre; — oder sie würde die Menge der Produktionen vermehrt, in deren Überfluß und dem Mangel der verhältnismäßigen selbst produktiven Konsumenten, gerade das Übel bestehet, das auf beide Weisen sich nur vergrössert. Es kommt hierin zum Vorschein, daß bei dem *Übermaße des Reichtums* die bürgerliche Gesellschaft *nicht reich genug* ist, d.h. an dem ihr eigentümlichen Vermögen nicht genug besitzt, dem Übermaße der Armut und der Erzeugung des Pöbels zu steuern."

❋ ❋ ❋

There is no need to give an explication of this text either. Its contents
are common knowledge, and from Marx to Keynes, from Disraeli to
our own time, economists and politicians have been grappling with
the same problem, seen from the same perspective. The inevitable
question, namely, what should be done, did not concern Hegel. He
was not an economist, nor was he a politician. He simply wanted to
describe the way things were and what it was possible, or impossible,
to do. But the results of his analysis have far-reaching implications.

What I have said about the relationship between morality and the
State ought to be sufficient to prevent a possible (and rather widespread) misunderstanding according to which Hegel was proposing
that morality and religion could resolve the social question. We can
show, however, that on this particular point his doctrine not only is
clear but is presented with a vigor rare even for an author who is not
in the habit of mincing his words: "It would be farcical and a bitter jest
[*Hohn*] to reject any animus that arose against tyranny with the remark
that the oppressed find their consolation in religion" (*PhR* §270, 258–
59; Knox, 165);[50] this is clear still in a State dominated by religion:

> With regard to how men should conduct themselves, what is
> enjoined is that there is no law for the just: simply be pious,
> and you can do whatever you like, you can abandon yourself to
> your own arbitrary desire and passion, and as for the others who
> thereby suffer injustice, you can commend them to the conso-
> lations and hopes of religion, or worse still, you can reject and
> condemn them as heretics. (*PhR* §270, 261; Knox, 167)[51]

50. "Wie es für Hohn angesehen würde, wenn alle Empfindung gegen die Tyran-
nei damit abgewiesen würde, daß der Unterdrückte seinen Trost in der Religion
finde."

51. "Für das Betragen der Menschen ergibt sich die Folge: dem Gerechten ist
kein Gesetz gegeben; seid fromm, so könnt ihr sonst treiben, was ihr wollt, — ihr
könnt der eigenen Willkür und Leidenschaft euch überlassen und die anderen, die
Unrecht dadurch erleiden, an den Trost und die Hoffnung der Religion verweisen,
oder noch schlimmer, sie als irreligiös verwerfen und verdammen."

For Hegel there is only the unconscious necessity of economic mechanisms, on the one hand, and the intervention of rational freedom, on the other. The need for intervention is all the more urgent in proportion to the severity with which the effects of these mechanisms have made themselves felt in a given society, because since society is the basis of the State, the latter cannot survive when it allows the former to decay. And this is precisely what is happening: "The disorganized condition of civil society turns on two of its moments: the sanctity of marriage and the honor of the corporation" (*PhR* §255, 239; Knox, 154).[52]

Without family, wealth, or the security that wealth provides, man can only reconcile himself to blind necessity if the State takes the place of the family. Without recognition of his social value, without his own place in the community of labor, man has no relationship with anything outside of himself and falls back into a state of nature and violence. Hegel understands this so well that for him the only State that can possibly be defined as "liberal" is the rational State. Only in a State where the citizen is satisfied will party propaganda be ignored, because propaganda relies for its effects entirely on the context in which it is received: "The veritable effect and danger [of propaganda] for individuals, society, and the State depends on the character of the [social] ground on which it falls, just as a spark is more dangerous if it falls on a heap of gunpowder than if it falls on hard ground, where it vanishes without a trace" (*PhR* §319, 328; Knox, 207).[53]

Society is well aware of the danger, but it cannot rise to the level of reason and still remain society. It can only place its faith in the economic system and try to use the State, thus revealing its utter incomprehension of how reason is embodied therein, to service the system's needs. The dialectic of this crisis then "drives bourgeois society

52. "Heiligkeit der Ehe und die Ehre in der Korporation sind die zwei Momente, um welche sich die Desorganisation der bürgerlichen Gesellschaft dreht."

53. "Übrigens . . . hängt ihre eigentliche Wirkung und die *Gefährlichkeit* für die Individuen, die Gesellschaft und den Staat, auch von der Beschaffenheit dieses Bodens ab, wie ein Funke auf einen Pulverhaufen geworfen eine ganz andere Gefährlichkeit hat als auf feste Erde, wo er spurlos vergeht."

beyond its limits—in the first place this specific society—to seek consumers outside of itself, and thus the necessary means of subsistence, in lands that are either lacking in the goods it possesses in abundance or in the general spirit of industry, and so on" (*PhR* §246, 233–34; Knox, 151).[54]

Hegel does not add "and then" to his "in the first place this specific society," but this does not make his meaning any less clear: the society in question—here he is referring to English society—will then adopt a policy of colonization; but once the other nations have become industrialized, the struggle for the world market ensues. This specific society, as it was phrased some hundred years later, then exports unemployment, even at the risk of conflict. Or else it undertakes unlimited expansion, and with it violent conflict; or it experiences social crisis, ending in the collapse of the State and the nation as autonomous and independent entities; or it enters the reign of reason, the satisfaction of all within and by the agency of the State: "Those peoples who could not tolerate or were afraid of domestic sovereignty have been subjugated by others, and their struggles for independence have brought them all the less success and honor as they found it less possible to create a rudimentary organization of the State—their freedom has died from the fear of dying" (*PhR* §324, 333; Knox, 210).[55]

One or the other, perhaps both one and the other; Hegel does not say. But he has said enough to allow us to decide. We know it well by now, this "mole," this "unconscious spirit," this passion that ensures that history does not come to a halt; we know what is lacking in the State to prevent its truly being what it claims to be: it *ought*

54. "Durch diese ihre Dialektik wird die bürgerliche Gesellschaft über sich hinausgetrieben, zunächst *diese bestimmte* Gesellschaft, um außer ihr in anderen Völkern, die ihr an den Mitteln, woran sie Überfluß hat, oder überhaupt an Kunstfleiß usf. nachstehen, Konsumenten und damit die nötigen Subsistenzmittel zu suchen."

55. "Daß Völker, die Souveränetät nach innen nicht ertragen wollend oder fürchtend, von andern unterjocht werden, und mit um so weniger Erfolg und Ehre sich für ihre Unabhängigkeit bemüht haben, je weniger es nach innen zu einer ersten Einrichtung der Staatsgewalt kommen konnte (—ihre Freiheit ist gestorben an der Furcht zu sterben—)."

to act ethically amidst the various forces playing themselves out in the international arena; it *ought* to ensure the satisfaction of all in the areas of recognition, security, and honor; it *ought* to . . . which means that it *is* not doing it. Reconciliation has not been realized between nations, nor has it been realized inside the State: at home and abroad it is the state of nature in all its violence that prevails, and the national, sovereign State remains as incapable of solving the larger problems of humanity as it is of solving the particular problems of men. The State, which *ought to* be stronger than society, *is* in fact weaker; the *concept* of man has not triumphed and replaced the *representation* of man; freedom has not conquered need.

✷ ✷ ✷

"The will of the many [*der Vielen*] overturns the government, and those who had formed the opposition until then take its place. But by the very fact that they now form the government, they are in the minority. This conflict, this nexus, this problem is the point that history has now reached, and the one for which it will have to find a solution in the times to come."[56]

A new form is coming. It is not for philosophy to say what it will be. At present, the real constitution of the modern State, that on which all our legal documents rely and of which they are, in the best possible case, nothing but the expression, is ailing. The remedy for the disease is to be found in the conscious realization of rational freedom, perhaps as the result of the action of some hero, some great man, certainly as the result of war, and thanks to the operation of the passions. It will also come from the State, that is, the State in its ultimately realized form, not in its present one, but necessarily *by means of* the present one since, however inadequate it might be, it is and remains the truth of its era. It will not be anarchy that saves humanity from local conflicts or those between States. The present State will disappear, but it will disappear in the same way that everything that has had posi-

56. *Philosophie der Weltgeschichte*, vol. 4, *Die Germanische Welt*, 933.

tive and *real* value has ever done, by a process of sublimation, thereby preserving everything in it that is (and has always been) rational.

The content of this unknown and unforeseeable form can therefore already be known and foreseen: the reconciliation of man with himself in the concrete universality of rational organization—rational in the sense that it is intended to safeguard the property of individuals as the concrete expression of their will (not to safeguard wealth, which is already in the process of being socialized in the present State), the family as the domain of feeling and human trust, morality as the inviolable sanctuary of conscience, and the national tradition as what gives life its direction and living substance. The future does not belong to the State, which dominates man, but to man, who will be truly man not despite the State but in the State, who will not be organized but who will organize himself, not to increase his power but to increase his freedom and the infinite value of individuality.

As yet it is uncertain what form this content will take; we cannot even guess at it. Nevertheless, the Spirit is working away in the "depths," and the people who represent it, whom it has elected as its chosen people at this point in time, will surely lose their supremacy hereafter: "The spirit goes beyond each of its properties as simple individual steps in its progress and submits this people to its chance and judgment."[57] The goal of history, supposedly attained already in

57. "Das Selbstbewußtsein eines besonderen Volkes ist Träger der diesmaligen Entwicklungsstufe des allgemeinen Geistes in seinem Dasein und die objektive Wirklichkeit, in welche er seinen Willen legt. Gegen diesen absoluten Willen ist der Wille der anderen besonderen Volksgeister rechtlos: jenes Volk ist das weltbeherrschende; ebenso aber schreitet er über sein jedesmaliges Eigentum als über eine besondere Stufe hinaus und übergibt es dann seinem Zufall und Gericht" [The self-consciousness of a particular people is the bearer of the present level of development of the universal Spirit in its actual being and the objective reality in which it has placed its will. Against this absolute will the wills of other particular peoples' Spirits have no rights; that people is the World Leader. All the same, however, the Spirit goes beyond each of its properties as simple individual steps in its progress and submits this people to its chance and judgment] (*Encyclopédia*, 3d ed., §550).

Hegel seems to have thought that the Russians would be the people destined to succeed the Germanic peoples. In the *Philosophy of World History,* after discussing the Latin and Germanic peoples he says, "Beyond these two great European orders there

the *Phenomenology of Spirit,* the World Empire of Spirit, remains to be realized, but the goal has not changed.

> States aim at independence, and that is considered to be to their honor . . . But independence is also to be seen as a purely formal principle . . . Each time that a State has been incorporated in another it has only lost its formal independence, but [without losing] either its religion, its laws, or the concrete [content] of its life . . . States tend, therefore, toward a general unity."

This unity is not domination, a hegemony in the Greek sense of the word: "here hegemony is spirit."[58]

----

is a third, the Slavic, which lives in a state of primitive solidarity [*in anfänglicher Gediegenheit*] . . . However, in regard to its foreign relations, it has already entered into the European system, specifically as a massive power that is the embodiment of hardness" (907). Undeveloped but firm and powerful, Russia has not yet displayed its full strength, which seems to suggest that the time has come for it to develop "its principle." He is more explicit in a letter to a Russian friend from Yxkull dated 28 November 1821, therefore contemporaneous with *PhR:* "You have the good fortune to possess a country that occupies such a significant place at the level of world history and to which, I am sure, is allotted an even higher destiny. The other States, it would seem, have already more or less reached the end of their evolution; perhaps many of them have already passed their highest point and reached their final form, whereas Russia, perhaps already the most powerful among them, bears within itself an enormous potential by virtue of its most intimate nature [*eine ungeheure Möglichkeit seiner intensiven Natur*]" (Rosenkranz, *Apologie Hegels gegen R. Haym,* 304).

58. *Philosophie der Weltgeschichte,* vol. 4, *Die Germanische Welt,* 761. Hegel is referring here to the Germanic States, and it is with them in mind that he envisages the principle of unification accompanied by a safeguard of freedom for historical individuals (i.e., States). But a bit further on he states that "with the arrival of the Christian principle the Earth now belongs to man . . . External relations no longer constitute the determinant factor; revolutions now take place internally." *Internally* means here inside the Christian world, which is for Hegel the whole world since with the appearance of the Christian principle of freedom and the infinite value of the individual man became the master of the Earth. The term *revolution* is an ambiguous one, though it does not seem that Hegel thought of revolution as much in the narrow sense (of internal politics) as in the principles governing the world, which come into being by means of war according to the Hegelian scheme.

It can also be noted that this idea of the Europeanized world was already present in Fichte (*Grundzüge des gegenwärtigen Zeitalters* [1806; Leipzig, 1922]), just as one can find there the concept of *Volksgeist* and that of the linear succession of spirits.

What is more, the arrival of this new form is not only necessary but close at hand.

> There is nothing new under the sun. But this is not the case for the sun of the spirit. Its trajectory and movement are not a simple repetition of itself but the changing exterior that spirit creates for itself in its ever-changing forms; this trajectory is essentially progress . . . By sublimating and suppressing and preserving [*aufheben*] reality, the existence of what is, it attains at the same time the essence, the thought, the universal of what it was as a mere existent . . . When spirit enters thus into itself, thought comes forth as a particular reality and the sciences are born. Thus sciences and the ruin, the disappearance, of a people are always associated with one another.[59]

Or as the *Philosophy of Right* puts it, "The completion of a process in which spirit apprehends itself is at the same time its externalization and the act by which it rises higher" (*PhR* §343, 345; Knox, 216).[60]

Is it *proof* that the hour is near that the birth of the new form is imminent? Yes, proof: the old form is obsolete because it is understood, because it could be understood, because it has given all that it could give. The Hegelian State dies—the proof of this is that the Hegelian philosophy of the State was possible. Because this form has reached its final stage, because it forced its way into reality, it must

---

It seems highly probable that Fichte had a considerable influence on Hegel, much greater than is normally supposed and in precisely those areas that are habitually thought to be characteristically Hegelian: Europe is for Fichte a single nation enjoying freedom in the *Christian-Germanic* era (ibid.). In an article on Machiavelli first published in 1807 (published in book form as *Machiavell* [Leipzig, 1918]) he teaches in the same way that (Kantian) ethics does not govern relations between sovereign States (an idea that goes back to Kant himself): *salus et decus populi suprema lex esto;* law and right have no power in this area. A remarkable analysis of Fichte's political thought that points out a number of other similarities (and differences) can be found in M. Boucher, *Le sentiment national en Allemagne* (Paris, 1947).

59. *Philosophie der Weltgeschichte,* vol. 4, *Die Germanische Welt,* 48. [This page number obviously is incorrect since p. 48 is part of the editor's introduction. TRANS.]

60. "Die *Vollendung* eines Erfassens ist zugleich seine Entäußerung und sein Übergang."

now stand aside, and Spirit, in its unconscious and subterranean labor, must move on toward a new *Wirklichkeit.*

**❈ ❈ ❈**

Yes, Hegel did justify the modern State, the State represented by the Prussia of his time; yes, it was Prussia that produced the consciousness of this stage in the development of spirit, of the realization of freedom. Yes, Prussia is justified inasmuch as it is the State based on thought—justified and by this very fact condemned. Spirit is preparing to take the next step. Hegel's awareness of this was so acute that he says it at the beginning of his *Philosophy of Right,* in a passage that is probably the most quoted of all of his texts and yet, it seems, one that readers are determined not to read. Here it is:

> Let us say one more word about this habit of giving recipes [instructing on] how the world ought to be. Philosophy, in any case, always arrives too late. As the thought of the world, it appears only when reality [*Wirklichkeit*] has finished its process of formation and is all done . . . When philosophy paints its grey on grey a form of life must have grown old, and it cannot be rejuvenated with grey on grey; it can only be understood. The owl of Minerva spreads its wings only with the fall of dusk. (*PhR,* xxiv; Knox, 12–13)[61]

A form of life has indeed grown old.

61. "Um noch über das *belehren,* wie die Welt sein soll, ein Wort zu sagen, so kommt dazu ohnehin die Philosophie immer zu spät. Als der *Gedanke* der Welt erscheint sie erst in der Zeit, nachdem die Wirklichkeit ihren Bildungsprozess vollendet und sich fertig gemacht hat. Dies, was der Begriff lehrt, zeigt notwendig ebenso die Geschichte, daß erst in der Reife der Wirklichkeit das Ideale dem Realen gegenüber erscheint und jenes sich dieselbe Welt, in ihrer Substanz erfaßt, in Gestalt eines intellektuellen Reichs erbaut. Wenn die Philosophie ihr Grau in Grau malt, dann ist eine Gestalt des Lebens alt geworden, und mit Grau in Grau läßt sie sich nicht verjüngen, sondern nur erkennen; die Eule der Minerva beginnt erst mit der einbrechenden Dämmerung ihren Flug."

*Appendix*

# Marx and the Philosophy of Right

Although an enormous amount has been written on Marx's relationship to Hegel, it has included few detailed studies and little unprejudiced work, at least to my knowledge and in the languages I know (the chief lacuna here being my ignorance of Russian). Such work faces great difficulties from the outset. Living in a Hegelian atmosphere, continually rereading Hegel's work, considering Hegel the last philosopher, Marx and Engels assumed that all their readers had a knowledge of Hegel, which in fact was already lacking by the time they reached the height of their influence. The critiques they made of Hegel rapidly became incomprehensible, and with few exceptions (such as Plekhanov and Lenin) Marxists have been satisfied to repeat these critiques without examining what they meant, what elements of the Hegelian system they accepted without reserve, and even what served them as the principle of any critique worthy of their predecessor. The "Liebknecht incident," mentioned earlier, is a good illustration of this failure.

I have no intention of resolving all these problems here, although their importance is only matched by their complexity. It is necessary, however, to ask in what manner Marx's thought differs from Hegel's. Historically it is because of Marx that Hegel has been influential, and in the consciousness of our time Hegel is more the precursor of Marx than Marx is the disciple of Hegel. Although it might be the case that the younger brother can only be understood with reference to the elder, it is the former who, directly or indirectly, is the main reason for the continued interest shown in the latter.

It is well known and has been repeated ad nauseam that the principal difference between the two is that one is an idealist and the other a materialist. This opposition takes on a more precise signification when the epithet *historical* is added to both terms. One can and must oppose a doctrine of history and historical action that teaches that the idea is all-powerful and a theory that sees in the external conditions under which men live the motive force of all change and progress. On the contrary, seen from a philosophical point of view the opposition loses any precise signification, whether the view is that of traditional metaphysics, which distinguishes idealism from realism and materialism from spiritualism,[1] or, *a fortiori,* that of dialectical philosophy, in which one of the traditional and predialectical abstractions transforms itself into the other. In terms of philosophical categories, we could say that Hegel and Marx were neither idealists nor materialists and were both one and the other.

Things are quite different when it comes to their political activities. In this area Hegel and Marx clearly part company. Hegel believed that understanding alone sufficed to realize the State of total reconciliation in the sense that the carefully considered actions [*l'action réfléchie*] of the present State authorities, that is, the administration, would do all that was necessary to prevent a rupture between social reality and the form of the State by guaranteeing the establishment of the kind of labor that would give to each citizen his family, his honor, his self-consciousness, and his share in the State, in other words, by guaranteeing total mediation. Marx, however, is convinced that only revolutionary action will be able to realize a truly human society in a truly human State.

Nevertheless it is evident given what has just been said about Hegel's political philosophy and given the decisive role that achieving

1. Karl Marx, *Aus der Kritik der Hegelschen Rechtsphilosophie* (1843), in *Marx-Engels Gesamtausgabe,* ed. D. Rjazanov and V. Adoratskij, 12 vols. (Frankfurt, 1927–35), vol. 1, pt. 1, cited below as *Critique,* e.g., "Corporations are the materialism of the bureaucracy, and the bureaucracy is the spiritualism of the corporations" (455) or "Abstract spiritualism is abstract materialism: abstract materialism is the abstract spiritualism of matter" (507). [For an English translation see Karl Marx, *Early Writings,* trans. Rodney Livingstone and Gregor Benton [London, 1992], 106 and 155. TRANS.]

consciousness [*la prise de conscience*] plays in Marx that the putative opposition between the two is extremely schematic. Hegel teaches us that it is real conditions that force the State (the administration) to act; Marx thinks and states openly that purely violent action is the contrary of progressive action, lacking as it does either a clear idea of its goal or *scientific knowledge*. This is a simple consequence of neither's adhering to an abstract philosophy of reflection but to a dialectical philosophy. In addition, for both it is unconscious action, or to be more precise, the simple feeling of un-satisfaction, that is the origin of all great historical events, and therefore achieving consciousness can only take place once the action has already gotten underway and will only be fully attained when the action has run its course. What is more, both are aware—Marx says it more clearly than Hegel— that achieving full consciousness of a historical situation indicates that this situation must and will be overcome,[2] just as both see the impossibility of drawing a precise image of the State to be realized, because only the meaning of the opposition to existing reality, not the new form that will be the result of present action, is determined. It is nevertheless the case that for one the stress is on the role of the masses (or the classes—both terms are found in Hegel and used in the same sense as in Marx), and for the other it is on government action. It follows from this that Hegel overlooked one of the most pressing problems of our time, namely, that one of the options open to the government is to favor one social class over the other. There is no doubt that he was aware that class conflict existed, but he did not attribute to it the importance it would rapidly assume in the ensuing struggle over the State itself (not simply *within* the State).  ·

The reason for this error of appreciation is clear (as are the causes: Hegel's having lived through a failed revolution, objective differences in the economic situation of both periods—Marx was thirteen years old when Hegel died, three years old when the *Philosophy of Right* was published, etc.). Hegel is a theorist, a *theoretician*, he is not and

2. See below, the discussion of the theory of the realization of philosophy and its suppression, as well as the theory of proletarian class-consciousness in the *The Communist Manifesto*.

does not want to be a politician. What interests him is the meaning
and direction of history in their totality, not the technical problem
of how to achieve the next step in the march of progress. It is of no
concern to him whether the liberation of man takes place now or
in a few centuries, whether it takes place here or elsewhere, in one
way or another; he is satisfied with understanding the nature of a
free society (it being as impossible for him as for Marx to predict its
concrete form). Marx—and here we do not need to point out how
much conditions had changed by comparing the Prussia of Frederick
William IV with that of Frederick William III, the European economy in 1840 with that of 1820, and so on—has no faith in the good
will of the government bureaucracy or its intelligence. Where Hegel
sees a problem for the government bureaucracy, Marx sees a struggle
between the ruling government bureaucracy and the oppressed class
(a term common to both Hegel and Marx); where Hegel bases his
analysis on the self-evident interest of the State, Marx places his hopes
for the future exclusively in the revolt of those who no longer have
family, morality, honor, or country. It is worth remembering that
Marx is not suggesting that we resort to violence for its own sake,
no more than Hegel. Marx too demands that political action have
a conscious direction, which he called the "revolutionary elite," the
"cadres," "the party," the "head" of the proletariat. But this new administration of things, destined to reconcile man with himself in a
new organization, whether one calls it the State or something else, all
the more so since Marx never developed a theory of the State, will be
created in opposition to the official administration instead of emerg-
ing from it by an imperceptible transformation of the constitution.[3]

3. "This [legislative] power is itself a part of the constitution that is presup-
posed by it, and thus it is in and for itself outside of its direct determination, but
the constitution receives its subsequent development with the development of the
laws and the progressive character of the general affairs of government" [Diese Gewalt ist selbst ein Teil der Verfassung, welche ihr vorausgesetzt ist und insofern an
und für sich außer deren direkten Bestimmung liegt, aber in der Fortbildung der
Gesetze und in dem fortschreitenden Charakter der allgemeinen Regierungsangele-
genheiten ihr weitere Entwicklung erhält] (*PhR* §298, 306; Knox, 193–94).

Another difference can be found in the fact that for Hegel the engine of history is war: a given State develops the newest form of the rational organization of freedom and enters into a struggle with the others in which it comes to be ultimately triumphant. In *philosophical* terms the reason for its victory is that it is the bearer of the idea, and in *material* terms it is that it can count on the patriotism of *all* its citizens.[4] On the other hand, for Marx it is not war that is a primary concern (it only becomes important with Lenin's attempt to develop a theory of imperialism) but the revolution within States, which would render the struggle between them superfluous.[5]

It is in his elaboration of the concept of class struggle that Marx transforms what for Hegel had been a *philosophical* concept into a fundamental *scientific* concept, and what is more, a concept at the limit of philosophy: passion. For Marx passion is the force that really drives history; it is, to use the language of the *Phenomenology of Spirit* (which Hegel will later discard), negativity as it appears to man in his history (i.e., for himself [*pour soi*]) and to the historian-philosopher in historical man (i.e., in himself [*en soi*]). For Marx this passion is determined at each stage of history, and this is no less the case for the contemporary historical situation. For Hegel only the passion that has been realized and has thus come to understand itself by determining itself is knowable scientifically, and in the eyes of the author of the *Philosophy of Right* the passion of any given present is nothing but a residue, a remainder to be assimilated by the self-consciousness

4. "This is the secret of the patriotism of the citizens in the sense that they know the State as their substance because it maintains their particular spheres, their right and their authority, in the same way that it looks after their well-being" [Dies ist das Geheimnis des Patriotismus der Bürger nach dieser Seite, daß sie den Staat als ihre Substanz wissen, weil er ihre besonderen Sphären, deren Berechtigung und Autorität wie deren Wohlfahrt, erhält] (*PhR* §289, 299; Knox 189). The *populace* therefore does not share in this patriotism.

5. "With the opposition of classes within a nation disappears the hostility between nations" (Karl Marx, *Manifest der Kommunistischen Partei*, in *Gesamtausgabe*, 6:543; for the English see *The Communist Manifesto*, ed. Frederick L. Bender [New York, 1988], 73). For Hegel equally it is the insufficiency of social wealth, therefore the (inevitable) crisis, that leads to expansionist policies.

of the historical-moral reality of the modern State (which becomes *real* in the administration). For Marx it is this very State that is the State of alienation, and not only is passion necessary in order to realize freedom but its tendency is determined by the concrete form of the reality in and against which it is unleashed. The lines of force that passion must follow if it wants to remain a passion for concrete freedom when it goes on the attack can be known scientifically. Once this is established, the subject and object of political action are immediately seen to be social (although Marx still situates them both within the framework of the Hegelian State) and thus allow a social science to be founded on political philosophy.

We can therefore say that all the elements of Marx's thought-action nexus are present in Hegel. They become scientific concepts and revolutionary elements from the moment Marx applies the concept of negativity developed in the *Phenomenology* to the fundamental structures [*données structurelles*] elaborated in the *Philosophy of Right*.

These two theses, or more accurately, these two attitudes, derived from the same demand, that of the satisfaction of man in and by the recognition of each and all and of each by all,[6] remain equally plausible to this day, and events cannot be said to have favored one over the other, although they have confirmed the common ground from which they spring: the necessity of man's liberation, which is in fact a conditional necessity, that is, a necessity only *if* one thinks that civilization, organization, and positive freedom should survive. The problems posed by the *alienation* of man, by wealth (not property in the Hegelian sense), therefore by capital, were clearly seen by both Hegel and Marx and have been recognized as being fundamental since their day by every reflective theory and political practice. That their solution is the main task of the present, just as it was that of Hegel and Marx's era, has been the most commonly accepted opinion for quite

6. The great merit of A. Kojève's book has been to place the concepts of recognition and satisfaction at the center of current Hegelian interpretation.

some time, but we have not come up with even a rudimentary political theory to account for all the new forms of the State that have sprung up since then.

Similarly, the apologists of peaceful evolution and those of revolution and dictatorship, as well as the critics of both of these political approaches [*procédés*], have all by and large been content to defend their personal opinions against those of their opponents with great passion and penetration but without deigning to examine seriously the inherent consequences of their own principles. We are tolerably well informed on how to incite or quash a revolution and how to institute and sustain a revolutionary or counterrevolutionary dictatorship, but we have barely bothered to ask what the strong and weak points of dictatorial systems or free democratic deliberation might be for the achievement of a desired goal, much less the role of the constitution and concrete ethics in a given nation (both terms, especially the first, being understood in Hegel's sense) when the possibility of following one or the other political approach is under consideration. The common agreement on their importance and the unanimous homage paid to words like *freedom, democracy, authority, law, equality,* and so on, simply demonstrate that the discussion is still mired in obscurity. To remedy this situation it would be necessary to begin by investigating the (conscious) coexistence of revolution, evolution, and reaction in the same world and then to look into the concrete meaning of the terms *formal* and *real,* one serving as a justification and the other as an insult, *both,* however, designating crucial realities or equally abstract moments of realities.

*  *  *

The sole purpose of the preceding remarks is to emphasize the difficulty of making a *comparison* between Hegel and Marx. They are by no means intended to offer an elucidation of the problem that was outlined, not even to suggest what might be required to fulfil such an aim. They were necessary so that we could speak very briefly of the *Critique of the Philosophy of Right,* written by the young Marx from March to August 1843.[7] I do not propose to analyze this text in any detail. If I wished to do so, it would be incumbent on me to proceed to a comparison between this critique and Hegel's theory and, given Marx's detailed gloss of it, to provide a paragraph-by-paragraph interpretation of the *Philosophy of Right.* I would then have the opportunity of pausing over certain of Marx's objections, some of which are particularly brilliant and well founded,[8] whereas others betray errors in the comprehension of its words and the theses it sets forth.[9] We shall have to leave this work to specialists who have made it their task to chart the evolution of Marx's thought. In the present context only the grand scheme, the principles of this critique, will concern us.

The *Critique* itself, unlike the *Introduction to the Critique of Hegel's Philosophy of Right,* which was published in Paris in 1844, has not excited any great interest. First published in Moscow in 1827, in the first volume of the Critical Edition of the Marx-Engels Institute, it did not draw much public attention even from the relatively select readership most interested in these matters.[10] Its tepid reception is quite comprehensible: the text is incomplete, ponderous, and difficult reading

7. For the date see D. Riazanov's preface to vol. 1, pt. 1, of *Gesamtausgabe,* lxxi ff.

8. For example, the critique of the deduction of the hereditary monarchy and the failure to consider the importance of wealth (capital) in the analysis of political conditions (although at this time Marx himself had not seen the difference between property and capital and so his critique remains less developed than the Hegelian analysis of *society*).

9. The most important of which is not to have seen that for Hegel the constitution is essentially historical and that the type he describes represents neither an ad hoc solution nor an eternally valid model.

10. See, however, J. Hyppolite, "Marx's Critique of the Hegelian Conception of the State," in *Studies on Marx and Hegel,* ed. and trans. John O'Neill (New York, 1969), 106–25. I regret to say that I disagree with the author's conclusions, mainly because of a difference in principle regarding the interpretation of Hegel. G. Gurvitch, "La sociologie du jeune Marx" (The sociology of the young Marx), in *Cahiers internationaux de sociologie* 4 (1948): 3 ff., is led to underestimate Hegel's influence on Marx because he fails to take into account the passages in which Marx acknowledges the fragmentary character of the *Critique.*

since most of the time it passes directly to the critique without troubling to give any prior textual interpretation, assuming on the part of the public a knowledge of Hegel that was probably justified in 1843 but is no longer the case today. In addition, his thought is, so to speak, pre-Marxist if one defines Marxist thought by the principles expressed in *The Communist Manifesto* and developed by Marx and Engels over the rest of their lives. Finally, the manuscript is not complete, not only because the first page has been lost but also because in numerous places Marx left blank pages that he intended to fill in afterwards, noting intermittently what precisions or additions he thought would be necessary at some later date.

But this is not the main point. The critique only deals with, and was only intended to deal with, right in the State, the Constitution.[11] So what the modern reader would consider to be of the greatest importance—the statement of Marx's position on the theory of society, on the one hand, and on the philosophy of history, on the other— is missing. Marx certainly had plans to take up the theory of society, but he did not carry them out in this manuscript. At the time he was writing the *Critique* he felt that a valid critique of Hegelian thought was possible on the purely political level. And on this level his critique is negative, although often justified. Not only does he not develop any positive theory of the State but he does not provide any indication that would allow us to ascertain the nature of his basic opinions on the subject. Certainly, he speaks of the preponderance of property *(Eigentum)* in this State, the opposition between man and citizen and this poorly camouflaged fault line that runs through the State and prevents the man's reconciliation with the State; he stresses that the administrative apparatus has taken over the State, that Hegel scorns democracy (a scorn Marx shares insofar as it remains purely formal democracy), and he critiques, with justification, the Hegelian deduction of hereditary monarchy. But none of these points ever attain the

11. See *Critique,* 497 ("We will have to develop this not here but in the critique of Hegel's treatment of civil society") and 499 ("The rest must be developed in the section 'Civil Society'") (*Early Writings,* 146, 148).

depth of his later views, which were to make their first appearance in the *Introduction* (published) to this *Critique* (unpublished). None of the fundamental concepts—real alienation of the human being, the class deprived of any participation in the historical community, even the concept of capital—appear in it. The language is that of Feuerbach; the term *critique*, characteristic of the group assembled around Bauer, appears often,[12] and the fundamental position is precisely the one that Marx criticize a little later, when he speaks of Feuerbach's "refutation" of religion: "Feuerbach dissolves the religious essence in the human essence. But the human essence is not an *abstractum* living in a singular individual. In its reality, it is the totality of social relations."[13] To summarize this critique, we have only to replace Feuerbach's name with Marx's and the term *religious* with *political* in these sentences. The doctrinal importance of the manuscript is therefore limited; in the final analysis it is of interest only for Marx's biography and the history of Hegelianism.

The significance of the *Introduction to the Critique* is quite different. The detailed critique has been replaced by the clear recognition that Hegel is *the philosopher*, the consciousness of the modern State. It is no longer a question of correcting some particular thesis or refuting faulty deductions. On the contrary, "We Germans are the philosophical contemporaries of the present without being its historical contemporaries . . . German philosophy of right and of the State is the only German history which is equal to the official modern present." "In politics the Germans have thought what the other peoples have done . . . It is in the head of the philosopher that revolution begins."[14] It is true that this was not the first time Marx paid such homage to Hegel; the manuscript of the *Critique* is full of expressions recognizing him as a thinker who accurately described a flawed reality.[15] But

12. See, e.g., *Critique*, 443, 446, 450 (*Early Writings*, 96, 98, 100), where Marx attacks Hegel for not carrying out a critique.

13. *Gesamtausgabe*, 5:535; *Theses on Feuerbach* §6 (*Early Writings*, 423).

14. *Zur Kritik der Hegelschen Rechtsphilosophie—Einleitung*, in *Gesamtausgabe*, I, pt. I: 612, 614 ff. (*Early Writings*, 249, 250–51).

15. See, e.g., *Critique*, 458 ("the Prussian or the modern State"); 487 ("Hegel takes his departure from the separation of 'civil society' and 'the political State' . . . this

whereas the manuscript is often hesitant, the *Introduction* makes its position crystal clear: "You cannot *aufheben* [suppress, sublimate, and conserve] philosophy without realizing it." This thesis finds its completion in another aimed at theoretical critique (Bauer, Feuerbach): "It [critique] thought it could realize philosophy without the *Aufhebung* of the latter."[16] Immediately following this Marx formulates the views that would be decisive for the development of his thought: saying that "revolutions need a *passive* element, a *material* basis" and that the revolution will only be fully realized as the accomplishment of the total liberation of man by "the creation of a class bearing radical chains . . . which, in a word, is the total loss of man and cannot therefore be regained except by regaining man totally. This dissolution of society as (= dissolution established in) a particular estate [*Stand*] is the proletariat."[17]

We are all familiar with what comes next: the development of a *technical* theory of revolution, the appeal to passion, organization of passion, the abandonment of any theoretical theory, the elaboration of economic categories derived from men in history and in relation to them, the fusion of politics and economics, the introduction of a historical index in every moral, economic, and political category — all of this because the Hegelian thesis is now accepted in its totality, because history has been given a precise meaning, that of liberating man *in reality* and not only in thought, because this total liberation and reconciliation have not yet been realized, because human relations still depend on passion, on the arbitrary, on chance, and on violence, because mediation has not been finally accomplished, because the struggle continues, and because existence is not yet rational.

---

separation, it is true, is a fact in the modern State"); 492, where Hegel is criticized for wanting to be satisfied with the appearance of reconciliation, but only after he had seen the contradiction; 502 ("the modern State of which Hegel is the interpreter"; "Hegel has often been attacked because of the way he interprets morality. He has done nothing more than interpret the morality of the modern State and of modern private right"); and 538 ("the flaw in the Hegelian interpretation and existing modern conditions") (*Early Writings*, 138, 144, 151, 177, 185).

16. *Introduction*, 613 (*Early Writings*, 250).

17. Ibid., pp. 615 ff., 619 (*Early Writings*, 252, 256).

This is not the place to ask where, how, and to what extent Marx, while accepting the essential content of Hegelian philosophy, moves beyond it, or more particularly what the famous expression "standing it on its head" means.[18] It is essentially a matter of extracting a *science* and a *technique* from a *philosophy,* of trying to realize something that was posited in philosophy as a purely hypothetical necessity and seeking the conceptual and political means that are available and indispensable to do it, of translating the idealism of philosophy (and of *any* theoretical science) into historical and political materialism. Is this passage from *philosophy* to *science* legitimate? Further, is it legitimate according to the principles of philosophy, which is required to give this science the validity and legitimation indispensable to its success? Or, on the contrary, does this transposition bring about an unreconciled and unreconcilable contradiction between the foregoing principles and their consequences? If this technical science can be elaborated (it does not seem to have been up to now, at least to any comprehensive degree), can we and must we draw conclusions about the character of the system underlying it? Or if it is a matter of understanding, must we not rather judge the pretensions of this science according to the teaching of the philosophy with which it openly associates itself? Can science endeavor to take the place of philosophy? Can philosophy, on the level of historical action, avoid being transformed into science or serving as a rationalization of passion?

We are under no obligation to answer these questions. It is nevertheless the case that the problems Marx is addressing are not contrary to Hegel's theses but in fact rely on them. The foundations of the sci-

18. [The reference is to Marx's comment on the Hegelian dialectic: in Hegel "the process of thinking" is turned into "an independent subject, under the name of 'the Idea,'" which is "the creator of the real world [which is] only the external appearance of the idea," whereas for Marx "the reverse is true: the ideal is nothing but the material world reflected in the mind of man, and translated into thought . . . The mystification which the dialectic suffers in Hegel's hands by no means prevents him from being the first to present its general forms of motion in a comprehensive and conscious manner. With him it is standing on its head, It must be inverted" (*Capital* [1873], 1:102–3, trans. Ben Fowkes, 2d ed. [London, 1977], postface). TRANS.]

ence that will liberate alienated man can be found in their entirety in Hegel. It is probable that, to quote Kant, we see the discoveries (of Hegel) as clearly as we do only because we have been told (by Marx) what to look for.[19] But it is still indisputable that it was in Hegel's writings that they were first to be found. And if we might be allowed to speculate, it seems very likely that Marx did indeed find them there himself. If there is an essential difference between the point of view of the *Critique* and that of the *Introduction,* was not his study of the theory of society in the *Philosophy of Right,* far more than the contacts he made with workers' circles in Paris, that was responsible? Is it not thanks to this influence that he opposes his dialectical theory to the French Communism of his time, which he considers to be a "dogmatic abstraction"?[20] In any case it is a fact that in the *Critique* Marx announces his intention to turn to the Hegelian theory of society after he has elucidated his theory of the constitution.

Whatever the truth of our hypothesis, it does not detract from Marx's originality (about which I spoke above) nor entail any "responsibility" on the part of Hegel. Hegel would probably not have approved of Marx's *science,* but this has not prevented it from being *one* of the historical translations of Hegelian *philosophy.* I have made these brief remarks because I believe that they might contribute to a better understanding of these two authors, to that objective understanding which alone permits us to take a position that is the expression of neither fidelity nor hatred, neither an instinctive preference nor an insurmountable aversion—an understanding that would amount to something different and more meaningful than a matter of taste.

19. Kant, "Über eine Entdeckung, etc.," in *Werke,* 6:1: "Allein wie viele für neu gehaltene Entdeckungen sehen jetzt nicht geschickte Ausleger ganz klar in den Alten, nachdem ihnen gezeigt worden, wornach sie sehen sollen" [However, as with many discoveries that supposedly have just been made, dim-witted expositors are merely seeing old ones clearly after having been shown where to look for them].

20. Marx to Arnold Ruge, September 1843, *Gesamtausgabe,* 1, pt. 1: 573 ("Letters from the Franco-German Yearbooks," *Early Writings,* 207).

*Library of Congress Cataloging-in-Publication Data*
Weil, Eric.
   [Hegel et l'Etat. English]
   Hegel and the state / Eric Weil ; translated by Mark A. Cohen.
      p.   cm.
   Includes bibliographical references.
   ISBN 0-8018-5865-8 (alk. paper)
   1. Hegel, Georg Wilhelm Friedrich, 1770–1831 — Contributions in
political science.   2. State, The.   I. Title.
JC233.H46W413   1998
320'.092 — dc21                               97-46838
                                                       CIP